The Which? Guide to Living Together

Imogen Clout

 CONSUMERS' ASSOCIATION

Which? Books are commissioned and researched by
Consumers' Association and published by
Which? Ltd, 2 Marylebone Road, London NW1 4DF
Email address: books@which.net

Distributed by The Penguin Group:
Penguin Books Ltd, 80 Strand, London WC2R 0RL

First edition April 2002
Copyright © 2002 Which? Ltd

British Library Cataloguing-in-Publication Data
A catalogue record for this book is available from the British Library

ISBN 0 85202 888 1

For a full list of Which? books, please write to
Which? Books, Castlemead, Gascoyne Way, Hertford X, SG14 1LH
or access our web site at www.which.net

Editorial and production: Joanna Bregosz, Alethea Doran, Liz Hornby, Nithya Rae, Barbara
Toft

Cover photograph: James Harrington/Tony Stone Images

Typeset by Saxon Graphics Ltd, Derby
Printed and bound in Great Britain by Creative Print and Design (Wales), Ebbw Vale

Contents

★ An asterisk next to the name of an organisation in the text indicates that the address can be found in this section.

This publication is a general guide to the law and should be regarded as such. Independent legal advice should be sought, tailored to the particular circumstances in hand. The authors will not accordingly accept liability for any loss or damage suffered as a consequence of relying on the information contained in this guide.

Introduction

People living together as though they are married do not fit comfortably within the law. In some respects they are treated exactly the same as married couples, but in others, such as pensions and inheritance, they are discriminated against. The legal position is awkward and unsatisfactory, and often cohabitants find out about it only when they are faced with a crisis in their lives such as bereavement or separation.

Urban myths about the position of cohabiting couples abound. The National Survey for Social Research, for instance, found in November 2001 that 37 per cent of the people they surveyed incorrectly believed that there was something called 'common law marriage' that gave cohabiting couples the same rights as married ones.

Lawyers are familiar with the unhappy consequences of people not having understood how the law would affect them. They hear cohabitants claim that, in a modern and enlightened society, they did not expect the law to differentiate between those who are married and those who are not, and between couples of the same or opposite sex. But, as the law stands, if you do not marry, children and partners can be left without adequate provision; cohabitants struggle to be recognised legally as next of kin; women who have lost their earning capacity and many years of pensionable employment find that they have no entitlement to compensation.

The law clearly recognises the position of a married person by giving the role legal status. This means that by defining someone as, say, a 'wife', one can immediately say what legal rights and duties that person has, simply because she is a 'wife'. However, a person who is unmarried but cohabiting is in an anomalous situation: he or she has no legal status as a general rule, although in certain areas of law, such as state benefits, the position of such a person is recognised. For the most part the law treats same-sex couples in the same way as it does unmarried heterosexual couples (even though this is not always true of social attitudes).

The purpose of this guide is to provide information about the legal position of people cohabiting as unmarried partners. It focuses mainly on those who are living (or intend to live, or have lived) in a relationship for a period of time, and suggests the best ways in which they can protect themselves, their property and any children, both throughout the period of the relationship, and also if it ends, whether by separation or by death. Unlike some books that have been written on the topic of cohabitation, it is not designed to deal with the position of any one particular group, such as women, or same-sex couples. It is not a manifesto for any group that feels that the law does not deal with them fairly.

The number of cohabiting couples is increasing rapidly. In 1996 the National Statistics and Government Actuaries Department found that there were about 1.5 million couples living together in the UK and estimated that it would double to 3 million by 2000–1. At the same time, the number of marriages is falling. Couples are cohabiting for longer periods of time and many are choosing to live together before they marry. Typically, cohabitants fall into one of the following categories: a couple who have no intention of marrying because they do not feel that marriage would be appropriate for them; a couple who are living together before they get married; or a couple who cannot get married, either because one or other is still married to someone else, or because they are a same-sex couple.

Marriage or cohabitation?

While marriage puts obligations on the parties, it has a number of advantages. The legal benefits of marriage are that spouses are treated as each other's closest relative (next of kin), and both have full parental status: this has consequences for matters such as tax, pensions and inheritance. If the marriage breaks up, the court has a very wide discretion in the way in which assets can be distributed between husband and wife, and the parties have rights to maintenance from each other: this means that both of them (and any children) should be properly provided for. This does not automatically happen if a couple is not married, and the court's powers to help are very limited. There are, for instance, no maintenance rights between former cohabitants. It is as though the law (reflecting traditional social views) states that if a couple is prepared to shoulder the legal burden of marriage, with all the duties and obligations that it implies, then the partners should have the benefits as well, in compensation.

A significant number of couples, mostly same-sex, wish to be married but cannot marry. The opportunity to register a same-sex partnership, recently pioneered in London, has, at present, no effect on the legal position of the couple. Proposals have been made that the law should be changed so that a registration of this sort would give a couple equivalent legal status to that of a married couple. Cohabiting couples – both heterosexual and same-sex – who might wish to take advantage of such a change in the law should consider carefully how a registration would alter their legal position.

By sensible planning and making the appropriate private arrangements, cohabiting couples can, if they wish to, achieve most of the legal advantages that a married couple would have in the eyes of the law. There are a few areas of law, notably in the field of taxation, where intractable problems could arise, but even then cohabitants can arrange their affairs so that they are not completely disadvantaged, and protect themselves as far as possible. As pointed out earlier, unless they make formal arrangements between them, they may find that they are treated almost as legal vagrants: they do not fit tidily into the legal system, and have a motley collection of legal remedies instead of a clear-cut position within the system. The paradox is, perhaps, that many couples will have avoided marriage precisely because they do not want to be bothered with paperwork and official recognition, only to find that this is precisely what they need if they are not to be disadvantaged before the law.

Changes in the air

While this book was being written, newspapers were full of stories about how cohabiting couples – both heterosexual and same-sex – were trying to change the law to win more recognition of their status. The Human Rights Act, which came into force in October 2000, has meant that such issues are being discussed with more urgency. However, the Act is not the panacea that it might appear to be. In a number of judgments the European Court of Human Rights has upheld the right of member states to preserve a distinction in their domestic law between the status of married and cohabiting couples. There is still a strong (and vociferous) lobby that argues that 'family values' must be preserved and that marriage lies at the heart of these. Any move, the argument goes, that gives cohabitation parity with marriage undermines the institution of marriage and the family.

Two bills are proposed for discussion in Parliament in early 2002, both intending to change the obligations and rights of cohabiting couples. These are private members' bills without government backing, so it is unlikely that either of them will become law; however, it is also true to say that Parliament will continue to debate these issues. As this book was going to press, amendments to the law on adoption were being proposed that would allow unmarried couples to adopt. In addition, some of the recent changes to the law relating to married couples – the

Child Support Act, pension sharing, and mediation in public funding – have affected cohabiting couples as well. The laws covering maintenance rights, inheritance rights and pension rights are all ripe for change. This book shows you how to take advantage of the turning tide and protect your interests even while the law is in a state of flux.

Differences in the legal treatment of married and cohabiting couples

This table sets out the chief legal differences between married and unmarried couples in England and Wales. It shows what steps the cohabiting couple can take, if they wish, to make their legal position more like – or, in some cases, identical to – that of the married couple, and what legal document(s) are needed for this. Some documents are essential for avoiding problems in the future, and are shown with an asterisk (*). The final column shows you where to find more information in the book.

Area of the law	Position of the married couple	Position of the cohabiting couple	What the cohabiting couple can do about it	What documents you need	Chapter
Inheritance and succession					
Inheritance	If one dies without a will (intestate) the other will inherit a large part or all of the estate.	No automatic inheritance rights when one partner dies.	Make a will. (Otherwise the survivor may have to make a claim under the Inheritance Act. This may be costly.)	*A will each.	5
Ownership of property and maintenance rights					
Property ownership	Even if the property is in the sole name of one spouse, the other spouse will have a right to claim a share (which may be more than 50%) on divorce.	Non-owner probably has no right to claim a share of property unless there is a written agreement or if 'trust principles' apply.	Clarify the rights of ownership in a document (which could be a 'living together agreement').	*A document setting out your property rights.	1 14

Area of the law	Position of the married couple	Position of the cohabiting couple	What the cohabiting couple can do about it	What documents you need	Chapter
Maintenance (for partner only, not children)	On divorce or separation either spouse can claim maintenance from the other if appropriate.	No rights to claim maintenance.	Nothing except by agreement. This may be difficult to enforce.	A living together agreement.	16
Rights of occupation	A non-owning spouse has a right of occupation of the family home.	No rights of occupation if a non-owner.	Non-owner can do nothing, except if he or she acquires an interest in the family home by gift or purchase.	In limited circumstances, an injunction to protect against violence.	14, 17
Ownership of chattels Liability for debts	If the marriage ends in divorce the court can adjust the ownership of all assets to achieve a 'fair' result.	No extra rights: you own it only if you paid for it, or if you received it as a gift or by inheritance.	Clarify who owns what and who will be responsible for what payments, in a living together agreement.	*A living together agreement.	2, 3, 15
Children					
Parental responsibility	Both parents have it automatically.	Only the mother has it automatically.	Make a parental responsibility agreement; or Marry; or Other parent can apply to court for an order.	A parental responsibility agreement (if appropriate).	4
Guardianship	On the death of one parent guardianship automatically passes to the other.	On the death of one parent guardianship will only pass automatically to another person who already has parental responsibility.	Appoint a guardian or guardians.	*A will (with guardianship included); or Appointment of Guardian.	12

Tax

	Married	Cohabiting	Action	See also	
Inheritance tax (IHT)	Spouse exemption means that anything transferred between spouses is exempt for IHT purposes.	No exemption is available.	Take legal/financial advice and plan giving in life and death as advantageously as possible.	A will. Deeds of gift in lifetime. Insurance policies.	5, 9, 14, 15
Income tax	Married couples allowance only for pensioners.	No tax allowance is available.	Nothing (but not much distinction between unmarried and married).		9
Children's tax credit	Available if a couple have children.	Same as married (except for same-sex couples who can claim two allowances if appropriate).	Claim allowance.		13
Capital gains tax	Spouse exemption means that anything transferred between spouses is free of tax.	No spouse exemption is available but can have two Principal Private Residence exemptions.	Take legal/financial advice and make use of personal exemptions. Plan giving in life and death as advantageously as possible.		9

Pensions and other financial matters

	Married	Cohabiting	Action	See also	
Pension	Generally there are rights as a widow/widower to claim a pension and/or a lump-sum payment on death of spouse.	Sometimes: depends on pension scheme. Some schemes do recognise a partner but less likely for a same-sex couple.	Check terms of scheme before you go into it. Nominate your death-in-service benefit in favour of your partner.	'Nomination' of scheme. Other savings schemes.	6

Area of the law	Position of the married couple	Position of the cohabiting couple	What the cohabiting couple can do about it	What documents you need	Chapter
Personal injury rights	Rights to damages for bereavement.	Limited rights (must have cohabited for two years) No rights for same-sex partners.	Make a will so that your partner benefits from the damages that are paid to your estate.	A will.	7
State benefits					
Child benefit	Available to adult caring for a child (generally paid to the mother).	No distinction between married and unmarried m/f couples. (Same-sex couples may be able to make two claims.)	No need.		8
Working families tax credit	Available to a family which is one or two adults with children.	No distinction between married and unmarried m/f couples. (Same-sex couples may be able to make two claims.)	No need.		8
Widow(er)'s benefit	Available if you were married.	Not available to a bereaved cohabitant.	Nothing. Life insurance could help.	A life insurance policy.	8
Widow(er)'s pension	Available if you were married.	Available if you were bereaved cohabitant.	Not available to a could help.	Nothing. Life insurance A life insurance policy.	8
Protection from violence					
Domestic violence	Available to married and unmarried couples.	Slightly less scope for unmarried couples and even more limited for same-sex couples.	No need in most cases. No extra remedies are available.		17

To the reader

What does living together – cohabiting – mean? One of the problems about living together, from a legal point of view, is that it is very often difficult to say at what point the 'living together' actually starts. Usually it is a gradual process: first the toothbrush left overnight, then the change of clothes, then the staying overnight for longer periods of time. In the end one set of parents invites you for Christmas and you know that you are, in the eyes of the world, a couple.

To count legally as living together you generally have to be living together 'as husband and wife', which is one of those legal phrases that reduces every family dynamic to a cliché of cosy living. Everyone is supposed to know what it means and it does not do to question it too closely. What it boils down to is living under the same roof (for most of the time), sharing a sexual relationship (for part of the time), and sharing a domestic life – cooking, eating, cleaning. Generally if you meet the phrase 'living together as husband and wife' in a piece of legislation, this will indicate that the law relates to a male/female couple. A number of pieces of legislation now refer to 'living together as a couple'. This implies that there is no distinction between same-sex or male/female couples. The same test of a shared domestic life would apply to both.

The various chapters of this book cover how you can create a legal relationship between you, in terms of children, property owning, inheritance and so on, and you will need to decide at which stage in your relationship it feels comfortable to do this. Readers of this book may be at various stages in their lives: you may be already in a long-term relationship, or thinking about it, or breaking up, or any of the various stages in between. The book is divided into sections that reflect the chronological progress of a relationship, rather than into sections that deal with the various areas of the law that you ought to know about. It ends with breaking up, although clearly many relationships will not end

A realistic view of life as 'husband and wife'

You don't necessarily have to have an ongoing sexual relationship to count as 'living together as husband and wife'. In the reported case of Miss Griffiths and Mr Watson, the couple had lived together for 30 years. During the last ten years of the relationship they had not slept together, but had shared the bathroom and living room.

He went out to work and she did the housekeeping, shopping, washing, cooking and gardening. The judge in the case said that it was not unusual for a happily married couple to abstain from a sexual relationship and they could be treated as living together as a husband and wife. This allowed Miss Griffiths to succeed in a claim under the Inheritance (Provision for Family and Dependants) Act 1975.

this way. (Indeed, one outcome of reading the book – and following the advice in it – may be that you will be able to form a stronger long-term relationship.)

Each of the three main parts deals with the issues that will be of most immediate concern to you if you are at this particular stage in your lives. However, the parts are not mutually exclusive and you will find it useful to read the whole book once you have dealt with your immediate situation. If you are already in a settled relationship it would be tempting to skip the first part about getting together: you have already done all that and may feel you don't need any more help with it. But it is worth thinking about whether you have made a proper agreement, or come to a settled understanding with your partner about the ownership of your home. If you have not done this, it is not too late to do it; the third part should alert you to the problems that may lie in the future if you do not deal with it.

If you are in a settled relationship it is also tempting to think that nothing will break it up and everything will continue to be rosy. But no one can predict the future, and death can end the most loving of relationships. If you have not planned for what may happen and taken steps to avoid the worst consequences of the law, one of you is going to have all sorts of problems to deal with.

The table on page 11 summarises the differences in treatment between married couples and cohabitants, and indicates what, if anything, you can do about them, and the chapters that deal with the issues.

The aim of this book is to reduce the misery that comes when people who have not understood (or not dealt with) their legal position find themselves unable to claim what they feel is fair, or at least not without a costly legal battle. It is not the place of the book to make moral judgements on people's lives, or to promote one sort of relationship over another. Loving, stable relationships, based on mutual trust and confidence, are good relationships. They are all the better if the people in them know how they fit into the legal framework of the society around them. A loving relationship does not benefit only the happiness, welfare and health of the couples; it has an outward beneficial effect on all that it touches, the children that it nurtures, the friendships that it fosters and the general benevolence that it extends to the world.

Part I

Getting together

When you fall in love, the financial and legal implications are the last thing that you normally worry about. To do so might seem unduly cynical or cold-blooded. Ideally you should be reading this book before romance, or passion, or lust takes over and completely clouds your judgement, as it invariably does. Lawyers see too many people who suffer the sad (and sometimes financially ruinous) consequences of not having been reasonably careful before they entered into a long-term relationship, living with their partner.

You don't need to be sceptical and suspicious; trust is an essential part of a loving relationship. But don't be naïve, either. Work out where you stand and what the legal implications are for you. And dare to think about the worst-case scenario: what will you do if you do not live together happily ever after?

One of the problems, legally speaking, about living together is that it can be hard to identify when it actually started. As your relationship becomes firmer and you both start to think of it in the long term, you will start to make arrangements jointly. Some of these joint arrangements will not have any long-term legal implications – you may go on holiday together, for instance, or split the bill at the supermarket. But once you start to buy property that you are going to keep, whether it is what lawyers call 'real property' – houses, flats and land – or things like furniture, or CDs, then the legal implications start.

Once you start to buy things that you refer to as 'ours' as opposed to 'mine', 'his' or 'hers', you need to consult the chapters that deal with that sort of property (preferably before you commit yourself to a purchase) so that you know what it entails. The same applies to making a contribution to your partner's property. If you are going to help repair or decorate your partner's house, for instance, or assist with the payment of bills, it is worth finding out whether this changes the property rights between you. You also need to think about this if your partner offers to contribute to your property: by accepting, are you giving him or her a claim over that property at a later stage?

The most important (because most valuable) issues to think about are your rights in the home that you share. You also need to think about the things that you buy together to go into that home and the ways in which you may support each other financially.

Chapter 1

Setting up home together

Once you begin to share a home it is not just your domestic arrangements that change: you are changing your legal relationship too. There are four main scenarios, each of which has different legal implications:

- one of you moving into a property already owned by the other
- one of you moving into a property already rented by the other
- buying a new property together
- renting a new property together.

Moving into a property owned by your partner

If you move into a property that is owned by your partner, you do not gain any rights in that property simply because you are living together. This means that if the person who owns the property chooses to sell it (or is forced to sell by, say, a mortgage foreclosure), you cannot stop the sale. By contrast, if you married, your rights of occupation would be protected by law.

The non-owner can gain an interest in the property (or in the proceeds of sale if it were sold) if you make a formal written agreement between you that you will share the property. If you own the property and are thinking of giving the non-owner a share of the property, then you need to read the section in this chapter on buying a property together, since the same considerations apply. The non-owner can also gain an interest in the property if he or she makes a contribution towards the purchase price, whether directly or indirectly, that he or she can prove is the result of an agreement that in return he or she would have a share in the property. (This does not have to be a written, formal agreement.) The law about this is described in more detail in Part III on breaking up; it is a complicated area of the law and there is considerable potential for litigation. This means that although one partner might acquire property indirectly, you will probably have to go through a legal dispute to sort out your rights in the property. This will undoubtedly be expensive, and stressful, and is something that you will want to avoid if at all possible. So the moral is to get your arrangements clear and in writing at an early stage in the relationship.

If it is not your intention to pass an interest in the property to the non-owning partner, it makes sense to express this in writing, by using a 'living together agreement' (see Chapter 3), or just the part of it that refers to the declaration that the non-owning partner accepts that he or she will acquire no interest in the property.

It can be difficult to have the sort of discussion that you need to have about what you both think about your interests in the property. However, if you do not talk about it you may find that you have each made different assumptions about the arrangements between you, and this can have disastrous consequences.

'Understandings' can lead to misunderstandings

Trisha, a teacher, had bought her own house and was paying her mortgage. She had a boyfriend for about three years. He started to stay overnight with her on two or three nights a week, but he did not want his mother to find out, and she never thought of herself as 'living with' him. He helped her with the decorating of various rooms and from time to time he bought things for the house, which she thought of as presents to her. Sometimes he helped her with the shopping. But the relationship soured and she felt that she must end it and persuaded him to take his things away from the house. He was very bitter and angry with her, and she was shocked to find out that he had gone to a solicitor and was making a claim to a share of the house, basing this on the fact that he had made a contribution to it by the work that he had done and the things that he had bought. He also alleged that they had been engaged, a fact which Trisha disputed hotly. He issued the claim at court and Trisha had to go to the expense of defending it. She was advised that he had a very weak case but it would cost money to defend it. In the end, she managed to persuade him to settle the matter on the basis that she paid him £1,000 to recompense him for his contributions. Though there was no evidence that she had promised him a share in the property in return for his contributions, there was no evidence that she had not. A record of an understanding that he would gain nothing in the property would have helped to avoid this situation.

Where the property is in the joint names of your partner and his or her spouse

The partner with whom you move in may be living in a property which is still in the joint names of him- or herself and a former spouse or partner. It could also be in his or her sole name, but be the subject of a claim by a former spouse or partner. The fact that you have moved in is an added complication from a practical point of view. As far as the law is concerned, the previous spouse or partner would have a much better claim in the property than you. This is particularly the case if your partner was previously married (or still is). Possession, in this situation, is not nine-tenths of the law. As the more recent cohabitant you rank a poor second to an earlier spouse.

Your presence may also make your partner's position a bit weaker, as your financial resources would be taken into account when the court looked at your partner's needs. This is not to say that you could be ordered to pay anything of your own to his or her former spouse, but if you were contributing (or able to contribute) to the family budget this might reduce the amount of income (or capital) that your partner needed to retain to maintain him- or herself. If you are not able to support yourself, your partner will still find it difficult to argue to a court that your new needs should take priority over those of his or her former spouse.

It may be prudent to postpone moving in together until your partner has sorted out the financial issues in his or her divorce. But your partner will still be asked in the course of the divorce proceedings whether he or she has any intention to cohabit now or in the future. If this question is asked and you do intend to cohabit, it is foolish to lie, as this could expose you to an application to overturn any final order. Your partner should tell his or her solicitor about what you intend, and take advice about the best way of dealing with the timing of it.

Moving into a property already rented by your partner

Your rights in a rented property will depend partly on whether it is a private rental or a council property. In Part III we look at your rights if your relationship breaks up, or the tenant dies. At this stage, where you are moving in together, you need to think about the legal relationship that you are creating.

The Which? Guide to Renting and Letting gives you detailed advice about your status as a tenant. This is a brief summary of the position of cohabitants.

Private accommodation

The first thing to check is that the tenant is not in breach of the tenancy agreement by allowing someone else to move in on a permanent basis. Most tenancy agreements will have a promise in them that the tenant will not allow another person to live in the property on a permanent basis, so you will have to talk to the landlord and get his or her consent to your being there if you want to do things properly.

You may be able to agree with the landlord that the person who moves in is added to the tenancy agreement or the rent book. If this is done, both of you will have equal status as joint tenants. This means that you will both be liable under the agreement for the rent and any other obligations. Your responsibility will be *joint and several* which means, as far as the landlord is concerned, that either of you can be made to pay the whole of any amount due. If your partner does not pay his or her share, you are legally responsible for the whole of the rent.

If the person who moves in is not given the status of a joint tenant then he or she will generally be treated in law as a licensee, which means someone who has the permission of the legal tenant to live in the property. This means that you have effectively no legal protection; if the tenant asks you to leave, you must go, though you should be allowed a reasonable time to take your things and move out. It also means that you do not have any protection against the landlord if the tenant leaves and the landlord wants you to go.

The tenant can also create a sub-tenancy (provided he or she is allowed to under the terms of his or her own tenancy agreement and by permission of the landlord, if required). You do not have to have an agreement in writing to create a sub-tenancy, though it is generally the best idea because it provides proof if there is a dispute later. The sub-tenant has to pay an agreed sum of money in rent and should have the exclusive right to occupy at least one room; it is not a very common arrangement between cohabitants for these reasons. If you create a sub-tenancy that is not permitted by your own tenancy agreement, this will give your landlord grounds for taking you to court, so it is inadvisable.

Council tenancy

Almost certainly your tenancy agreement will require you to get permission for your partner to move in, though the council should not refuse their consent unreasonably. Don't risk breaching the terms of your agreement and giving the council grounds for possession proceedings. The position of the person who moves in with permission is slightly more secure in a council tenancy; the tenant may be able to assign the tenancy and the tenancy can also be inherited. This is described in more detail in Chapter 14.

Buying a new property together

There are two ways of owning 'real property' jointly in English law, and it is crucial that you understand what the differences are. (Lawyers use the term 'real property' for houses, flats and land.) For most everyday practical purposes it makes no difference how you hold the property, but the crucial differences emerge when one of you dies, or you split up, and this can cause a crisis, so it is important to get it right at the beginning of the ownership.

The two different ways of owning property are:

- joint tenancy
- tenancy in common.

The word 'tenancy' in these two legal expressions does not have anything to do with renting the property; it simply means that you 'hold' or 'own' the property.

If you hold property under **joint tenancy** you are each treated as holding an equal share of it, but the shares are not regarded as being two separate entities. If one of you dies the other will inherit the deceased's share automatically. You cannot leave your share of the property to anyone else in your will.

If you own a property in your sole name and you decide to share it with your partner, by putting it into joint names in a joint tenancy you have effectively made a gift of one half of the property to your partner. (You could later bring evidence to show that this was not what you had intended to do. However, as you will see in Chapter 14, the law is complicated, sorting out your interests would be an expensive process, and it would be better to avoid the problem in the first place by being explicit about your interests in the property.)

If you want to hold property under a **tenancy in common**, you can state in the transfer documents when you buy the property that you intend to hold it in unequal shares: say, 60:40. It would be appropriate to do this if you contribute unequally to the purchase price and want to make sure that if you split up you get your fair share. If you do not specify the shares in which you hold the property, then the assumption is that you hold it equally.

Unlike in a joint tenancy, the shares of a tenancy in common are divisible, in the proportions that you have specified, and you can leave your share to anyone you like in your will. It will not pass to your partner automatically on death.

Pros and cons of a joint tenancy

A married couple (by way of comparison) will normally choose to hold their home as a joint tenancy. This means that if either dies the other will inherit the home without any need for a will and their equal positions reflect the shared enterprise of marriage. If you feel that you are both making an equal contribution to the purchase of the home, and you want your partner to have it on your death, a joint tenancy may be for you. If you are the partner who is putting in the smaller share, or nothing, a joint tenancy will mean you have been made a gift of half the home from the outset.

Pros and cons of a tenancy in common

At the outset of a joint venture such as the purchase of a property, you may feel uncertain about a commitment that gives your partner half of everything (particularly if you are contributing the larger share). It may be better, from your point of view, to have a tenancy in common, so that your unequal contributions are reflected in the shares in which you hold the property. This may also be the case if your family (or both your families) are helping you with the purchase by giving or lending you money. If you do hold the property as a tenancy in common in unequal shares, a court is unlikely to rearrange the shares in the property if you later split up (although it might postpone the sale of the property). (See Chapter 14.)

There are a couple of difficulties with this position, however. It can be difficult to assert your view to your partner without looking as though you do not trust him or her. A good conveyancing solicitor, faced with an unmarried couple who want to buy a property, should explain the differences in the ways that you can hold the property, and should be concerned to make sure that if you are putting in money in unequal shares you get proper advice, individually, about the implications of what you are doing. If you do not receive advice from your solicitor along these lines, you should seriously consider finding another solicitor.

The other difficulty is in quantifying what a contribution actually is. It is fairly common for one partner to have capital and the other income. If one party puts a lump-sum payment into the purchase price and the other pays the mortgage, how are you going to rate one contribution against the other? At first, the mortgage payer will have contributed nothing to the equity of the property, but as time goes on and the capital owing is reduced, the mortgage payer may have contributed more than the person who paid the lump sum at the beginning. You also need to consider, if you have the sort of arrangement where one of you pays the mortgage, that the other may be buying other things, such as groceries for the household.

Sorting out your agreement

These questions call for some rational discussion and fairness on both sides. It may be sensible for you each to consult a solicitor. A family mediation service may also be prepared to facilitate a discussion for you. If you feel that you are being pressurised or manipulated, you will need to think very hard about the nature of the relationship that you are creating.

If you decide that a tenancy in common is best for you, your conveyancing solicitor should draw up a document called a 'declaration of trust'. This should set out what each of you has contributed to the purchase of the property; you can also say in it what contributions you intend to make towards the household; and you can state what you will do in the future if one of you wishes to sell the property and the other does not: for example, you can include arrangements for one to buy out the other's share. The declaration of trust should be kept by you or your solicitor with the title deeds, so that you can refer to it if you ever need to in the event of a dispute.

Make a will

If you buy property as tenants in common, you should both make wills to provide for what is to happen to your share of the property on your death.

Getting a mortgage together

From a legal point of view there should be no difference between a husband and wife getting a mortgage and another two people getting a mortgage, but in practice you may find that various mortgage companies will draw a distinction.

The problem is generally not with the mortgage, but with the insurance policies that go with it. If you have an endowment mortgage, this is backed by a life policy designed to grow in value and pay off the mortgage when it gets to full term. If you have a repayment mortgage, you may still be asked to take out life insurance if you borrow a particularly large proportion of the value of the property or take out a particularly large loan. Life insurers treat 'single' men, in particular, whether gay or straight, even if they are in long-term relationships, as being riskier, with the particular focus being on HIV. Same-sex male couples may face the most difficulty. Some firms quite overtly refuse to insure same-sex couples, or will insist on additional questions being answered. It would be tempting to conceal your sexuality or your relationship, but if you do it gives the insurance company grounds for repudiating the policy completely. This is because insurance agreements are meant to be made with the 'utmost good faith' on both sides.

Your best option may be to aim for an ordinary repayment mortgage, without a requirement for an insurance policy. (Endowment mortgages have, in any event, had poor press in the past few years.) If you think that an endowment mortgage would best suit your needs there are helpful websites that can assist you in searching for the best mortgage and insurance deals. These are listed at the back of this book.

Changing a joint tenancy into a tenancy in common

If you start off with a joint tenancy and decide later that you want to change into a tenancy in common, you can 'sever the tenancy'. You cannot, however, use a similar process to turn a tenancy in common into a joint tenancy. You may feel that you want to sever the tenancy because of your relationship together, or you may be advised to do this if you have business commitments that require you to give a personal guarantee. Take legal advice before you do this, so that you are in a position to consider all the implications fully. If this is done unilaterally, the split will always be 50:50, irrespective of the contributions to the purchase price made by you and your partner, unless the latter agrees to a different split.

Either of you can sever the tenancy at any time by giving a notice of severance to the other. This can simply take the form of a letter from you, signed and dated, stating:

> 'Please accept this letter as notice of my wish to sever as from this day the joint tenancy in our property known as [insert the address of the property] now held by us as joint tenants both at law and in equity so that from this time onwards the said property shall belong to us as tenants in common in equal shares.'

You should ask your partner to sign the letter as an acknowledgement that he or she has received it and then put the letter with the deeds of the property. Also, if the land is registered (which is most often the case), a restriction must be entered on the register to protect the interests of the person doing the severing.

If you do sever the tenancy you should both make wills, either at the same time or as soon as possible after the severance, because you will no longer automatically inherit each other's share.

Renting a new property together

A tenancy agreement that you enter into together will treat you both as tenants of the property and put you on an equal footing. It does not, however, mean that in law each of you is responsible for only half the rent, even though this is what you may have agreed between you. You need to be aware that you will be *jointly and severally* liable for the rent, and any other obligations under the agreement. This means that if the landlord cannot pursue one of you, he can pursue the other for the whole of the obligation. While you are living together in prosperity and harmony this is unlikely to cause you a problem; but you need to be aware of the potential difficulties if you split up.

If you decide that only one of you will take the tenancy, make sure you know the position of the non-tenant (see *Moving into a property already rented by your partner*, above).

Chapter 2

Other joint arrangements

Sorting out the ownership of your home, and your interests in it, is obviously the biggest issue from a legal point of view because of the value of the property. But there are a number of other points to think about at this stage. If you get them sorted out early on in your relationship it can save misunderstandings and problems later on.

Insurance for household contents

When you move in together, you need to think about insurance arrangements. If the one who already lives in the home has existing contents insurance, you cannot assume that the other partner's possessions will automatically be insured under that policy. You will need to speak to the insurance company and explain the situation. Some companies will automatically treat a cohabitant as a member of your 'family' and cover his or her possessions as well.

If this is not the case you will need to take out a policy in your joint names, so that there can be no argument about the extent of the cover. A number of insurance companies state that they would make no distinction between a policy covering a married or unmarried couple, and there would be no distinction, either, if the cover was for a same-sex couple.

Car insurance

If you drive each other's car you will obviously need to arrange for your car insurance policy to cover this. Most insurance companies will charge a higher premium for an unmarried couple than for a married couple because they say that, statistically, unmarried people have more accidents! Do not be tempted to say that you are married when you are not because, if you needed to make a claim, this would give the company grounds for refusing to pay, on the basis that you had not been truthful to them.

You may find that you get a better rate if the main driver is a woman, but you will need to shop around for the best deal.

Council tax

Council tax is charged on the basis of a two-person household, so if you are a single person you get a reduction on the overall charge. The bill may be in just one person's name (traditionally it was in the man's name, as head of the household), but joint tenants and joint owners are 'jointly and severally' liable for the payment of the council tax. (Councils refer to the 'liable owner', although 'liable occupier' would be a more accurate term, since in practice it doesn't matter whether or not you own the property.) You are also liable if you are the partner (in this context not a same-sex partner) of the 'liable owner' (even if you are not the owner of the property yourself), or if you are a non-owning resident of the property.

This all sounds very complicated; what it boils down to is that if you share the property you share the liability for council tax. You cannot argue that you are only responsible for your half of the account.

Water rates

Even if only one partner has his or her name on the bill, the water supplier has the power to pursue any occupier of the property for the payment if the named person does not pay. If you are an adult living at the property you could be liable. This simply depends on your residence, not your relationship.

Bills for utilities

Utility bills (for gas and electricity) used to be issued only to a single, named head of the household. These days most companies will issue a bill to you in joint names, if this is what you want. The named person is the person with the legal responsibility for paying the bill. However, if he or she does not pay, the gas and electricity companies have statutory powers that allow them to pursue any adult occupier (and consumer), so you could find yourself liable. Joint names on the bill will, as with the other legal responsibilities that we have looked at, make you 'jointly and severally' liable for payment.

TV licence

You need only one licence for a household, so one of you needs to have the licence in your name. If you have two homes, you need two licences. If someone in the household qualifies for a free licence, such as someone who is over 75, then the whole household can have the benefit of the exemption.

Credit cards

Your liability depends on whose name the card is in. If it is in your name, even if you have another named user, then you alone are liable. Only if the card is in your joint names are you jointly liable, and then you will be 'jointly and severally' liable.

If you buy something for your partner on your credit card, you are still liable for the payments for it, even though you do not treat it as your property, and even if your partner has promised you that he or she will make the payments. The credit card company are not interested in your private arrangement; they will simply pursue the card holder.

Chapter 3

Living together agreements

Chapters 1 and 2 will have shown you that it makes a lot of sense to think about the legal implications of what you are doing when you decide to live together. You can formalise any joint decisions in a 'living together agreement', or you can simply discuss the points that such an agreement highlights. With nothing written down, it can be hard to remember, much later, what you have agreed to; or one person's recollection may be very different from the other's. A written record (even if it is not a formal legal document) should help avoid arguments.

Living together agreements are a comparatively recent development in the law. This means that there are not many precedents and the style of them is developing and changing as more people start to use them. (The Solicitors Family Law Association★ is working on a set of precedents for living together agreements which should be available to its members during 2002.)

Living together agreements also have a rather ambivalent status in the law. It used to be said that they were void, for reasons of public policy: because they encouraged immorality. Nowadays a court would be unlikely to state this view in these terms. But it might be reluctant to enforce an agreement for other reasons – broadly speaking, the attitude of the courts is that you cannot sign away rights that the court would give you, because to do so would be to undermine the authority of the court. For instance, if you sign away your right to claim maintenance for a child, you cannot be held to that agreement if you need to claim maintenance at a later stage.

That might make the whole idea of a living together agreement seem a waste of time. It isn't, for several reasons.

- An agreement is extremely useful as evidence of what you both agreed to, particularly if you later have a dispute over what shares in the family home you are entitled to.

- If you draw one up *in the form of a deed*, it is binding in the way any legal contract between two parties would be. This means that if you need to you can sue for breach of agreement. This would be a last resort, but the knowledge of the status of the document should help resolve disputes.
- Though not binding upon a court, an agreement would generally be persuasive, particularly if you have both had legal advice about the implications of the document before you signed it.
- Perhaps most importantly, an agreement will help you to think about the things that might otherwise later give rise to arguments. If you can do this at the outset of your relationship, it is likely to be healthier and happier.

What can the agreement contain?

The answer is almost anything. Some American agreements go into exhaustive detail about who will take the rubbish (trash) out and which evening a week the parties will devote themselves to 'enjoying each other'. As there are no legal constraints, and very little legal tradition of such agreements, you can feel free to put in whatever you want. As a general guideline, however, keep the agreement simple and short. You want this to be easily understood, unambiguous, and enforceable. You can always have a separate, non-legal list of household chores or evenings of pleasure that you stick up on the fridge and adapt as time and circumstances dictate.

The essential points that you need to think about are listed in the box.

How to draw up an agreement

Using the list in the box, and the sample agreement at the end of this chapter, try to discuss the things that you would want to put into an agreement. You may feel that it would be helpful to take some legal advice, and that is strongly recommended if you are going to share in the purchase of a property, or if one of you owns the intended family home and the other is going to move in. Obviously you will have to pay a solicitor for a first appointment and, if you want the solicitor to draw up the agreement, for the work that that involves. The solicitor should be prepared to see you both for a discussion, but if he or she feels that there is the potential for a conflict of interest between you he or she will be obliged, because of professional rules, to say that you should be separately advised. The typical situation which would cause a solicitor to give this advice would be where one of you owns the home and is proposing to give the other an interest in it. (See Chapter 1.)

Living together agreements: essential points

- Who owns the home? If it is jointly owned, in what shares?
- Is the non-owner going to acquire any share in the property?
- Will the same arrangements apply if you buy another property together?
- How are household expenses to be met?
- Who is going to pay for what?
- How are you going to buy things for the house, and who is going to own them?
- Do you want/intend to have children, and will you need to renegotiate the agreement if this happens?
- If you have children, together or from previous relationships, how are they going to be supported?
- What events might bring the agreement to an end, or mean that it would have to be renegotiated?
- If the property is in one partner's name, what security will he or she provide for the other if s/he dies first?
- What arrangements will you make if your relationship ends?

Since solicitors generally charge on a time-related basis, you will reduce the costs of taking legal advice if you have already discussed most of the points that you want to go into the agreement, and if you can take with you a rough draft of what you want it to say.

If you feel that you can manage without a solicitor you can write out your own agreement. If you want this to have the status of a 'deed', so that it becomes a legally binding agreement, you will need to make sure that it is formally signed by both of you. Your signatures should be witnessed; you may not witness each other's signatures, but another person can witness both your signatures. (You no longer need to stick a red legal seal by each signature, as you may have seen on old legal documents.) Keep the original document somewhere safe and keep a photocopy each, just in case.

Alternatively, you can simply note the essential points that you agree to. If you both signed this, without formalities, it would still be a useful evidential document, though you would not be able to sue if your partner did not keep to his/her side of the bargain.

If you make a really good job of coming to an agreement you may never need to look at the document again, because you will already have resolved the issues that can otherwise cause you problems later on. However, remember that if your circumstances change you may need to check to see whether it still reflects what you both want and need.

Revising the agreement

One of the chief difficulties about drawing up any living together agreement is that life is full of changes that you cannot always anticipate. An agreement that is entirely suitable when you are both young, healthy, childless and in full-time employment may not suit at all when one of you loses his or her job, or when you have a child. Your agreement needs to anticipate some of these factors and consider what you might want to do. However, try to keep the broad principles simple. If you do not do this you may feel that the task of drawing up the agreement is overwhelming, simply because of the impossibility of providing for every eventuality.

You can decide, for instance, that you will revisit the agreement every five years and decide whether it still expresses what you want. You can also provide in the agreement itself that it will be renegotiated in the event of one or other of you being out of work for a long time, or if you have a child. It is vital that you do renegotiate it if you find yourselves in a different situation from the one that you had first anticipated: if your contributions to the household change, for example.

Changing circumstances

Elizabeth and Douglas drew up a proper agreement when they set up home together, buying a house with the aid of a mortgage. But soon after they bought the house Douglas changed his job and could no longer pay his share of the mortgage. So Elizabeth agreed to pay the whole amount. However, they did not revisit their agreement and three years later, when they split up, Elizabeth found that she had a legal battle on her hands. She had made all the contributions, the house had increased in value, and Douglas was claiming that he was entitled to half the proceeds of the sale, because that was what the agreement said.

In the end, Elizabeth succeeded in paying him far less than half, but only after an expensive battle, with solicitors involved on both sides and a great deal of stress and unpleasantness.

Even if you have a solicitor draw an agreement up for you, you should not feel that the agreement has a life of its own that it imposes on you. If you both feel that it needs rewriting, then you can do that. It is not a straitjacket; it is meant to be of help to you in the future.

Using the sample agreement

The sample living together agreement that follows should help you think about what you might want to put in an agreement for yourself. As far as possible the sample is written in non-legalese, though it does contain some formal legal terms, particularly when it comes to dealing with property law.

When you have worked out which clauses you need, replace '#' with the number of the clause, starting with 7. Rows of dots are for your names, as appropriate in each case, or other obvious insertions. Square brackets [ ] indicate other places where words need to be inserted, or where there are alternative clauses that you might want to use.

Living Together Agreement

THIS DEED OF AGREEMENT is made the [insert day deed is signed, e.g. 14th] day of [insert month] 200[year]

BETWEEN: (1) [insert the full name of one partner] of [insert address] (' [insert a short way of referring to this person in the rest of the document] ')

AND: (2) [insert the full name of one partner] of [insert address] (' [insert a short way of referring to this person in the rest of the document] ').

WHEREAS:

1. .... and .... intend to live together.
2. .... and .... wish to enter into an agreement regulating their rights and obligations towards each other.
3. .... and .... intend that this agreement shall be legally binding upon them.
4. .... and .... have declared their financial positions to each other as set out in summary form in Schedule A at the end of this deed.
5. .... and .... have no children at present.

or

5. .... and .... already have a child/children, called [insert their full names and dates of birth].

and/or

5. .... already has a child/children from a previous relationship, called [insert their full names and dates of birth].

6. .... and .... intend to live at [insert address of the family home] ('the Home') which is a [purchased/rented] property in the [joint/sole] name[s] of ....
.... AND .... AGREE as follows:

#. *The Home*
The Home is vested in the [sole/joint] name[s] of .... and ....
[as a joint tenancy/tenancy in common] [in equal shares/in shares of ...
% to .... and ... % to ....] [and despite any contribution which
.... may make directly or indirectly towards the purchase maintenance or improvement of the Home s/he has and will acquire no beneficial interest whatsoever in the Home].
[......... has contributed £ ...... and .... has contributed £ ...... to
the purchase price of the Home.]

#. *Purchase of another property*
If the parties decide to sell the Home and purchase another property for
themselves the proceeds of sale of the Home will be applied as follows:
– to repay the mortgage to [insert name of mortgage lender]
– to pay the estate agent's fees for sale
– to pay the solicitors' costs of sale
– to pay to [insert any other debts that should be paid out of the proceeds]
AND any remaining balance shall be used for the purchase of a new
property which .... and .... will hold in [equal] shares [shares
of ... % to .... and ... % to ....].

#. *Endowment policy*
In the event of the current mortgage being redeemed the proceeds of
the related endowment policy with [name of company] shall [be shared
equally] [remain ....'s alone and s/he may choose whether to
cash it in or continue to keep it going].

#. *Outgoings*
.... and .... will open a bank account at [insert name of bank and
address of branch] ('the household account') into which they will each
contribute [equal] monthly sums [by standing order] from their
personal accounts on the [insert day, e.g. 1st] day of each month. The
following household bills will be paid by the household account:
water rates
council tax
gas
electricity

telephone
television licence
television/video rental
buildings insurance
contents insurance
mortgage repayments
endowment payments
rent
food and household necessities
decoration of the Home
repairs to the Home
ground rent and service charge
items of furniture and equipment for the Home.

[......... will pay for .... and .... will pay for ....]
Either party may draw cheques on the account with[out] the signature
of the other.
If items are bought with money from the joint account they shall
belong to .... and .... jointly in equal shares unless they agree
otherwise [in writing] [and list them at the end of this deed].

#.   *Contents of the Home*
All items of personal use or recreation belong to the person who last
acquired them whether by inheritance, gift or purchase.
All items of property owned by each person before they lived together
shall remain that person's sole property unless expressly given to the
other person.
All items of property purchased by funds from the household account
or purchased by joint contributions from .... and .... will be
shared equally between them.

#.   *Cars*
The car [make and registration] registered in the name of .... is the
property of .... alone, and despite any contribution by .... to its
maintenance, repair or running costs, will remain the property of
.... alone.
A similar clause can be used to cover any other large item of property where you want to
make ownership clear, such as a boat.

#.   *Pensions*
.... and .... shall each nominate the other to receive ... % of the
pension and death-in-service benefits to which each may be entitled
under any pension scheme from time to time.

Either shall be free to cancel such a nomination if this agreement terminates for any of the reasons set out in clause #.

You can also insert clauses about:

- wills
- insurance policies (for each other or for Inheritance Tax liability)
- enduring powers of attorney (see Chapter 5)

#. *Termination/Variation*

This agreement shall terminate if any of the following events occur:

- the death of .... or ....;
- the marriage of .... and .... to each other;
- notice in writing given by one party to the other at which point the transitional provisions set out below shall apply;
- .... and .... ceasing to live together at which point the transitional provisions set out below shall apply;
- one party leaving the Home and the other party treating this as ending the relationship at which point the transitional provisions set out below shall apply.

#. *Transitional provisions*

In the event of this agreement being ended except by death or by marriage of .... and .... to each other, the following transitional provisions shall apply:

- both .... and .... shall cease to contribute to the household account;
- any balance in the household account shall be divided equally between .... and ....;
- any debts that have been jointly incurred and are outstanding shall be paid jointly by .... and .... and they will indemnify each other in respect of these debts;
- any items of household furniture or equipment that have been jointly acquired as described above shall be divided between .... and .... either by calculating the value of each of the items by taking its purchase price and allocating them between .... and .... equally or by one of them purchasing the other's share so as to achieve as equal a division as possible;
- .... will forthwith leave the Home (except as set out in the final sub-clause below);
- .... will pay to .... a sum equal to [one half] of the increase in value of the Home (if any) from the time when they began to live together (which present value is agreed by .... and .... to be £ ......) until the time when .... leaves the Home. A valuation

of the Home will be obtained from a local valuer jointly chosen and instructed by .... and .... and if a charge is made for the valuation the cost of the valuation will be paid by them equally. If .... and .... cannot agree about a valuer the President of the Institute of Chartered Surveyors should be asked to appoint a valuer for the purpose;

- .... will pay the sum referred to above on or before six months from the date when .... vacates the Home;

- .... will undertake to make appropriate arrangements so that in the event of his/her dying before .... his/her executors or personal representatives shall allow him/her a period of six months in which to vacate the Home.

#. *Reconsideration and renegotiation*

Once .... and .... have lived together for a period of ...... months/years they will reconsider the terms of this agreement and vary them if appropriate.

This agreement will be reconsidered and renegotiated if .... gives birth to a child.

Any variation of this agreement shall only be effective if recorded in a further written agreement executed by both .... and ....

IN WITNESS of this agreement the parties to the agreement have signed it as a deed on the day and year first shown above.

SIGNED AS A DEED by the said [insert full name of first person]
in the presence of:

[here a witness should write his/her name]

[witness's signature]

[witness's address]

[witness's occupation]

SIGNED AS A DEED by the said [insert full name of second person]
in the presence of:

[here a witness should write his/her name]

[witness's signature]

[witness's address]

[witness's occupation]

Schedule A

We have declared our present financial positions to each other as follows:

[insert first person's name]:

Income:

Gross salary £ ...... per year; net salary £ ...... per month.
Any other income: £ ...... per year/month arising from ......
Capital:
house/flat: value of equity £ ......
savings: £ ......
shares: £ ......
car: £ ......
contents (and personal possessions): £ ......
other: £ ......
Debts:
mortgage: £ ......
credit cards: £ ......
credit agreements: £ ......
loans: £ ......
other: £ ......

[insert second person's name]:
Income:
Gross salary £ ...... per year; net salary £ ...... per month.
Any other income: £ ...... per year/month arising from ......
Capital:
house/flat: value of equity £ ......
savings: £ ......
shares: £ ......
car: £ ......
contents (and personal possessions): £ ......
other: £ ......
Debts:
mortgage: £ ......
credit cards: £ ......
credit agreements: £ ......
loans: £ ......
other: £ ......

Schedule B
Write down any property which is one person's over which the other
will acquire no property rights whatsoever.

Schedule C
A list of property that can be added to during the course of our relationship and that we will share jointly:

Item	*Price*	*Date bought*

Part II

Living together

Once you are established as a couple, the fact that you are not married may not impinge very much on your day-to-day lives. Your parents may find it difficult to find a way of describing your relationship to other people, but this may be the only awkwardness that you encounter. It would be tempting to feel that there was nothing else that you needed to do to sort out your legal position. To some extent you are right; but there are some precautions that you need to take to avoid possible crises later on.

If you have children, you will need to think about your legal position as parents, which is set out in Chapter 4. There is nothing that you can do in advance, but once a child is born, you will need to consider what is legally called 'parental responsibility'.

You will also need to think about your financial position in the future, and in particular (though it may seem rather morbid) what will happen when one of you dies. It is essential to think about making a will, each of you. And you should do this at a fairly early stage, even though – especially if you are both young or not very well off – you feel that you have little to leave at this stage except your debts.

This part of the book also sets out information about pensions and insurance, and what rights you have to be treated as your partner's nearest relative – next of kin.

Chapter 4

Children

The Children Act 1989 sets out the law about children. If any issues about children have to be decided by the court, the welfare of the child is regarded as the paramount consideration. The Act got rid of the old legal terms and concepts of 'custody', 'joint custody' and 'access'. It is no longer correct, or accurate, to use these terms, although you will find journalists still use them. The legal position is that when a child is born, the mother automatically has 'parental responsibility'.

Parental responsibility

'Parental responsibility' means all those rights and duties that go with being a parent. Typically this would include:

- the duty to care for the child
- the right to consent to medical treatment
- the duty to educate the child properly
- the right to choose a school for the child
- the right to decide on the child's religious upbringing
- the right to choose what name the child shall have
- the right to apply for a passport for the child

but this list is not exhaustive.

The unmarried father of a child does not have parental responsibility automatically. He can get it after the birth in three ways, one of which is by marrying the mother. Assuming that this is not the option you choose, the other ways are:

- to enter into a parental responsibility agreement (described below). This is possible only if one parent is the father of the child. It is not an option, for instance, for a lesbian couple

- to make an application to the court for an order; you might need to do this if you are the father and the mother dies. An application to court is not necessarily a hostile move; but there might be conflict if the mother opposed the application.

The Adoption and Children Bill 2001, which at the time of writing is being considered in Parliament, contains a clause which would give an unmarried father parental responsibility if he registers the child's birth together with the mother. The present arrangements for registering a child's birth are set out later in this chapter.

Applications under the Children Act 1989 are described in Chapter 12.

Are there any pitfalls in sharing parental responsibility?

Mothers who have to make the decision whether or not to share parental responsibility with fathers can easily feel as though they are being asked to give something away, or submit themselves to control or interference from the father, by doing it. However, this is not the case. Parental responsibility is primarily about the adult's relationship with the child; it is not diluted or eroded by being shared. Each person with parental responsibility is entitled to (and mostly will) exercise the rights and duties independently of the other. This reflects the reality of parenthood; parents do not normally have to consult each other about every daily decision concerning their children. It makes sense to make the big decisions about the child's life (such as schooling) together in any event, whether you share parental responsibility or not. If a mother with sole parental responsibility acts without consultation, she could provoke the father into making an application to the court to challenge her decision, which is a situation that you would want to avoid.

If you feel that you are in a stable relationship then it makes sense to share parental responsibility; it gives formal recognition to your partner's place in the child's life. You may, however, have misgivings if your partner seems to treat the idea as giving him a right of ownership of the child, as if the child were an object rather than a person. Parental responsibility does not confer possessive rights. If your partner says that he wants parental responsibility because he wants to feel that he owns the child, you may need to discuss (if you can) the whole idea of being parents together before you commit yourself to making an agreement.

Once you have made a parental responsibility agreement you cannot take it back; only a court can alter parental responsibility after the agreement is made, so it is a serious step that you should think hard about. It would be sensible for both of you to take some legal advice from an experienced family law solicitor. The Solicitors Family Law Association,★ which exists to promote good practice and expertise among its members, keeps lists of local solicitor members. The Law Society★ can also tell you about local members of its Family Law Panel.

Do we need to share parental responsibility?

Sharing parental responsibility probably has more emotional consequences than legal ones, on a day-to-day basis. In most situations in real life, if you say that you are the father of a child, you are unlikely to be asked about your legal status. The Children Act 1989 says that a person with parental responsibility may arrange for some or all of it to be met by one or more persons acting on his or her behalf. This means that the children's mother can delegate responsibility to her partner. Also, the Act specifically states that any person who has care of a child may do what is reasonable in all circumstances for the purpose of safeguarding or promoting the child's welfare. In an emergency, for instance, the unmarried father could give consent to medical treatment.

However, Department of Health guidelines on consent do make it clear that only a person with parental responsibility can legally give consent to the treatment of a child, so in some circumstances you might find that you were actually asked a question about your technical status. There may be some situations where having parental responsibility will give you an added authority that will help you.

The most important circumstance in which you will need parental responsibility is if the child's mother dies, or becomes unable to care for the child. If you have not acquired parental responsibility by agreement before the death of the child's mother, you will have to apply to the court for an order giving it to you. This will take time, there will be legal costs, and you will have a worrying time even if it is unopposed. (See Chapter 12 for a description of procedure.)

Parental responsibility agreements

A parental responsibility agreement can be made only by the child's actual father and mother. It has to be made on an official form; you can get a copy of the form from a law stationers (look in *Yellow Pages* under 'Legal stationery' for your nearest one), or download it from the Court Service★ web page on the Internet. The instructions on the back are quite clear and helpful. You will need one form for each child. You have to fill it in in black ink (so that it can be photocopied successfully). Once you have filled it in you need to go to a local court, either the magistrates' court or the county court, and sign it in front of a court official who will witness your signatures. The form tells you the documents that you will need to take with you to prove your identity.

Once you have both signed the agreement, you must make two copies of the front page (you do not have to copy the notes) and send it to the Principal Registry of the Family Division at the address shown on the form. You do not have to send any fee with it. They will register the agreement and send each of you a stamped copy of it.

Keep the agreement safely, as it is the official proof of your status. If you lose it you can apply to the Principal Registry for another copy. They will charge a fee of £1 if you know the registration number and £20 if you don't.

Sharing parental responsibility with someone who is not the father

There are some cases where you may wish to share parental responsibility with another adult who is not the child's father. This would arise, for instance, in a lesbian couple, where one has had a child but both intend to bring the child up as its parents. Sharing parental responsibility will give the other partner legal status towards the child, as well as recognising the role that that partner is going to play in the child's upbringing.

You cannot share parental responsibility by making a parental responsibility agreement as outlined above, as this is restricted to the child's actual mother and father, but you can do it by asking the court to make a 'residence order' under section 8 of the Children Act 1989. This automatically brings parental responsibility with it. (A person who is not a child's natural parent cannot just have parental responsibility by itself.) The application has to follow the standard procedure (described in Chapter 12), up to the first 'directions appointment' (the first court appointment, at which the future progress of the case is sorted out). If the judge is satisfied at that first hearing that the order will be in the best interests of the child (and nobody opposes it) he or she will normally make the order.

A judge might, faced with the case of a same-sex couple who wished to share residence and parental responsibility, order a court welfare report, in order to be satisfied that this would be in the child's best interests. There is no legal authority to suggest that there is any inherent harm that will come to a child from an upbringing by a same-sex couple. A number of cases make it clear that the court should not be prejudiced against a same-sex couple.

Appointing a guardian

Immediately after the birth of a child, especially if you have not done so before, you should make a will. If you have already made a will, you should update it. Making a will, and the reasons why it is especially important if you are not married, are set out in Chapter 5.

You can appoint a guardian in a simple signed document, without going to the lengths of making a will and it is sensible to think through who you would like to appoint before the baby is born, and to check with the people you choose that this is something they would be happy to do.

A new baby: why wills need to be changed

Tim was six months old when both his parents were killed in a road accident that he survived, thanks to his car seat. His parents, who had made wills before his birth, had not updated them since his birth and nobody was appointed to be his guardian in the event of their deaths. The result was a legal battle between his parents' respective families who both felt, for their various reasons, that they were in the best position to look after him. In the end the judge decided his mother's parents' home would be the best place for Tim, but the legal battle had been costly and he effectively lost touch with his father's family because they were so upset by the decision.

To avoid the sort of situation that happened in Tim's family you can use the form of wording in the box below. Be sure to sign and date the document and put it in a safe place. Tell the people whom you have appointed and give them a copy of it too. It would also be sensible to tell other family members, who might assume that they would take responsibility for your children on your death, so that you avoid the potential for a quarrel.

Wording for the appointment of guardian(s)

In accordance with section 5 of the Children Act 1989 I appoint [insert name(s) of guardians] of [insert address(es)] to be the guardian[s] of my child[ren] [insert the child(ren)'s names].
Signed:
Name: [print your name]
Dated:

Registering a child's birth

Rather surprisingly, the registration of a child with a particular name, or with a father's name, does not give the father any more status. (However, as mentioned earlier in this chapter, the law on this is likely to change.) Nor is the birth certificate conclusive proof that a person is the child's father. It simply raises what lawyers call 'a rebuttable presumption'; that is, a statement that is assumed to be true but can be disproved.

Who has to register the child's birth?

The responsibility for the registration is the mother's. The birth should be registered within 42 days (six weeks) of the baby being born. You have to go to the local register office, ideally for the area in which the baby was born, but you can go to another office if it is more convenient and the registrar will send the details on to the right office. Some maternity hospitals have arrangements with the local register office, so that the local registrar comes round to your bed and takes the details from you.

You can put the child's father's details on the register if:

- he comes with you to the register office and you both sign the birth register
- he does not come with you, but instead fills in a statutory declaration acknowledging that he is the father (you can get this form from the register office in advance of the registration)
- you have already made a parental responsibility agreement and you take this along to the register office. In this case, the father can register the birth without the mother having to be there.

Also, if the mother cannot go to the office with the father, she can sign a statutory declaration acknowledging that he is the father. (This form is also available from the register office.) In this case, too, the father can go alone to register the birth. If you can't make any of these arrangements to include the father on the birth certificate – which might happen, for instance, if the father is abroad at the time of the birth – then you can include his details at a later date, if you wish, by re-registering the birth. The local register office will be able to help you arrange this.

Choosing the child's surname

The person who registers the child has to tell the registrar what forename(s) and surname the child is to have. You can decide what surname the child is to have; it does not have to be the father's (even if he is on the birth certificate). Equally, you do not have to obtain the father's consent to the use of his surname. The giving of a father's surname is not evidence of paternity, any more than the birth certificate itself. Many couples these days, cohabiting or married, are choosing to give their children a double-barrelled surname composed of both their surnames, particularly if the woman has not changed her name to the man's. This can result in some rather indigestible mouthfuls, but the choice is up to you. You can change a child's surname at a later stage, but if you share parental responsibility this should not be done by one of you on his or her own; one partner can ask a court to stop the name change. (Chapter 10 deals with changing your name.)

Adoption

You may want to have children just as much as any married couple and consider adoption if you are unable to conceive. If you are not married, you may feel that you start off with insuperable difficulties, and this may feel even harder if you are a same-sex couple. But there are adoption agencies that will place children with unmarried couples and same-sex couples, and the government has made it clear that this in itself should not be regarded as a barrier to adoption. In a recent survey carried out for the British Agencies for Adoption and Fostering★ (BAAF), it was found that cohabiting couples were more likely than married couples to consider adoption. BAAF has campaigned for cohabiting couples in long-term stable relationships to be able to adopt as couples and 68 per cent of those they surveyed agreed with this idea.

BAAF has a useful website with information about how to go about adoption. This has links to the very informative Department of Health website.★ This in turn has links to a list of Voluntary Adoption Agencies all over the UK. Many of them include a description of the sort of children they place and the people that they are looking for to adopt them.

At present your legal position is different from that of a married couple: a cohabiting couple cannot adopt a child *as a couple*; the law allows only married couples to adopt. There are changes in adoption procedure coming into the law in the Adoption and Children Bill, which will probably come into force in 2002. This may change the law about adoption for cohabiting couples so as to permit a couple who are both over 21 and in a stable relationship to adopt. As this book went to press, it was not certain whether same-sex couples would be included in this change. The legal position at present is that if you want to adopt a child, one of you has to be the adoptive parent and then the other parent is granted a residence order, which allows you to share parental responsibility. The adoption agency will, however, look at both of you as a couple before deciding whether you are suitable as parents. BAAF publishes useful guides to the procedure that you have to go through. Stonewall★ also offers advice for same-sex couples.

Following adoption by one parent and a residence order to you both, in all day-to-day arrangements you would therefore be treated as the child's parents and the non-adoptive parent would not have a 'second-class' status.

There would be a key difference between the two of you as parents in inheritance law, however. If you do not marry, the adopted child is the adoptive parent's next of kin. An adopted child ranks equally with any natural child of its parent, and can inherit if the parent dies without a will. He or she would outrank the other (non-adoptive) parent in terms of inheritance. But if you are the parent who only has parental responsibility for the child, the child is not treated as any blood relative of yours in inheritance law and will have no rights to inherit from you. Again, this would be a crucial reason for making a will.

If you separate, only the adoptive parent is legally responsible for the maintenance of the child. This contrasts with the child born to unmarried parents, where both parents have a duty to maintain the child.

Stepchildren

One or both of you may have a child from a previous relationship. You will often be called that child's stepfather or stepmother, but if these terms are used in law (which is fairly infrequent) this applies only to *married* step-parents. The status of the unmarried step-parent is even more tenuous in law than that of the cohabitant. In this section, the term 'stepchild' is used to refer to a child from your partner's former relationship who lives (mainly or partly) with you and your partner, and 'step-parent' refers to you in your relationship with that child – even though these are not legal terms.

Maintenance

An unmarried step-parent has no obligation in law to maintain a stepchild, either during the relationship or once you have separated. This means that the Child Support Agency★ cannot pursue you for maintenance for the child if you split up with the child's parent. See Chapter 16.

Parental responsibility

You cannot, either, have parental responsibility for your stepchild by a parental responsibility agreement, as described earlier in this chapter, as this is available only to the child's natural parents. However, if you have a stepchild who lives with you and his or her true parent, you may be playing a much bigger role in the child's life than the non-resident parent. In that case it may seem to you and your partner that sharing parental responsibility would be appropriate. If this is the case you can apply to the court for an order giving you shared residence with your partner, as this will bring parental responsibility with it. All applications under the Children Act 1989 follow the same general procedure, whether opposed or 'by consent' (this is outlined in Chapter 12). If the child has another parent living who also has parental responsibility (generally, this would be where your partner was married to him or her), you should try to obtain his or her consent to the application, and he or she would have to be notified of it. If you cannot get his or her consent, this parent might oppose the application, but the court can decide what seems to be in the best interests of the child.

If the child has a father living who does not have parental responsibility (because he was not married to the child's mother) he does not (technically) have to be served with a Children Act application. However, if he has any contact with the child the court would probably order him to be notified, so it would make sense to do it at the outset.

Inheritance

Your stepchildren will not be treated as your kin in inheritance law, so they would have no rights to inherit from you if you do not make a will. However, if you have supported them and they are dependent on you for financial support (both during their childhood and once they reach the age of 18) then they might have the right to make a claim against your estate under the Inheritance (Provision for Family and Dependants) Act 1975. It may seem odd that stepchildren have this right if the step-parent dies, but not when a cohabiting relationship breaks up and the adults are still alive; but that is how the law stands at present. You will need to take legal advice about how you can deal with this in your will.

Chapter 5

Inheritance

It is in the area of inheritance that the law makes the harshest distinctions between married and cohabiting couples. If you die without a will, English law provides for automatic inheritance only by your spouse and your blood relatives. It is therefore vital that you make a will if you want to provide for your partner after your death.

Why a will is essential

Look at the intestacy chart at the end of this chapter to see where your property will go if you die without a will ('intestate'). If you do not have a spouse (or you are divorced), your children will take the estate, and if you have no children then your remoter relatives will take it. Your partner will not inherit anything from you if you do not leave a will, although he or she may be able to make a claim for some provision from your estate as described under 'Claims if you are left unprovided for', below. By making a will you can prevent the worst consequences of leaving your partner unprovided for. Otherwise, if the home is in your name and you die first, you may leave your partner homeless; if you are the major breadwinner, your partner may have no means of support. Your children will be the people who inherit from you. This can create the awkward (and sometimes very hostile) situation of stepchildren evicting their step-parent, or even adult children pitted against their own mother (or father).

A 'living will' is a different kind of document, explained in Chapter 7.

What happens if you die together

This is a minor point of law, but it can worry some people. If you die in the same accident and the order in which you died cannot be proved (this is very rarely the case because of the forensic tests available) then the law says that the younger is treated as surviving the elder. If you both die without wills this raises no issues, because you would not inherit from each other in any event. If you have wills and have left your estates to each other the younger would inherit from the elder, so that the elder's property would become part of the younger's estate. You can arrange for this not to happen by providing that you each must survive the other by a specified number of days (usually 28) before you can inherit.

For Inheritance Tax, if the order of death cannot be established, you are treated as dying at the same time.

Children vs. parents: a battle to avoid

Anna says: 'Simon and I lived together from when we were at university. We never saw the need for a piece of paper to say that we were committed to each other. We never made wills either, because we never realised that there was any need. But Simon died when he was 55 and the house was in his sole name. This meant that it went to our son James. You would have thought that this might not be a problem, but I'm afraid that James and I have not seen eye to eye for years and I don't get on with his wife. I think she must always have wanted to get me out of the house. So I had to get a solicitor and it cost a lot of money that all came out of the estate that Simon had left. In the end they did agree to give me part of the money, but I've had to move to a really poky little flat and there's no hope of ever having a family relationship again.'

Cost of making a will

It is possible to make a will for yourself, and you may have seen forms that you can get to fill in. However, the risks of getting it wrong are considerable, as a will is a technical legal document. As a cohabitant, you have a complicated legal situation, especially if you have children, and you should use a solicitor to draw up your will. The costs involved if you get it wrong far outweigh the cost of having a will drawn up properly.

Most firms of solicitors will prepare a will for you for a fixed price, and will offer to do a pair of wills, one for each of you, for a price that is less than the cost of two separate wills. You can phone solicitors to get a quotation for a price. The standard price may well be varied if you need advice on Inheritance Tax or Capital Gains Tax and tax planning, or where you have complicated family situations.

It makes sense for you both to make wills at the same time, although you cannot always organise this. Often your two wills will mirror each other:

... in the event of Mary dying first she leaves all her property to George and appoints him her executor ...
... in the event of George dying first he leaves all his property to Mary and appoints her to be his executor ...

Lawyers call these 'mirror wills'. ('Mutual wills' involve contracts to leave property to each other and are a different proposition.)

Public funding for wills

Public funding, described as 'Legal Help' (which has replaced what used to be called the 'green form scheme' under the Legal Aid system) is available to cover the cost of making a will if:

- you meet the financial criteria, *and*
- you are aged 70 or over, *or*
- you are disabled, *or*
- you have a child who is disabled, *or*
- you are a single parent (which in this context means unmarried) with a child under 18 and you want to appoint a guardian for your child after your death.

Public funding is administered by the Community Legal Service,* which is a division of the Legal Services Commission.*

Don't let the idea put you off

It is easy to get quite upset when you begin to contemplate making your will. Some people feel quite superstitious about the idea. It is almost as though you feel that the prospect of contemplating your own death can hasten the evil day.

Making a will is easier than you think

Katharine says: 'I'm a solicitor and I ought to know better, but it took me ages to get round to making my own will. Every time I thought about it, it really depressed me. I thought about all the people I would be leaving behind and I was overwhelmed by the complication of it. But in the end I got another solicitor to do it and it was really easy with his help. He helped me through all the complications and I now feel much more secure. If you have a partner, or children, you owe it to them not to leave a horrible mess behind you.'

Before seeing the solicitor

Before you go to see the solicitor, make a list of all the property that you own at the moment, and any that you know you are likely to acquire in the foreseeable future. List your debts as well.

The solicitor will need to know about your family and dependants (people whom you support). It may help if you can draw a family tree. Give some thought to the way in which you would like your estate (the property that you will leave) divided. Think too about who would be the best people to appoint as your executors (the people who have the legal responsibility for sorting out your estate after your death). Most executors will instruct solicitors to help them deal with their legal duties, and the task is responsible but not unduly difficult or time-consuming. Banks advertise that they will be your executors, but generally this means that the charges to the estate will be greater than they would be if you appointed individuals, even if they use a solicitor to help them deal with the administration of the estate. Your own firm of solicitors can also be appointed to be your executors. If you appoint a solicitor as your executor he or she will be able to charge at professional rates for the service that he or she carries out as the executor, but this is likely to be cheaper than the charges that banks will make. Generally you do not need a professional executor and a single individual can carry out the task. But you may feel that there will be family difficulties after your death and it can be helpful to have two executors, one of whom can bring some detachment to the task.

Checklist of information to take to the solicitor

It will save you time (and therefore money) if you make a list of the following details before you see the solicitor.

- Your personal details, and those of your partner:
  - name
  - address
  - dates of birth
- Children's names, dates of birth, and addresses if they no longer live with you
- Names and dates of birth of any stepchildren you support
- Name and address of any ex-spouse
- Your wishes about cremation, burial, funeral and so on
- Names and addresses of the people you want to be executors and/or trustees (see 'Trustees for your estate', below)
- Any particular legacies that you want to leave, with the names and addresses of the beneficiaries

- How you want to divide the rest of your estate, with the names and addresses of the beneficiaries
- Approximate value of your home and the amount(s) of any outstanding mortgage(s)
- Details of any life insurance policies: company, policy number, amount due on death
- Information about your pension arrangements: company, reference number, death benefits
- A list of all your major assets, such as savings, TESSAs, PEPs, ISAs, valuable possessions, shares
- A list of all your major debts.

It is often easy to think about who needs to inherit most of your estate, but you may find it difficult to remember all the little bequests that you might like to make, of things like keepsakes for close friends. Don't let this put you off making a will. You can add a note of your wishes about smaller items of property later if you provide for this in the terms of your will; your solicitor can advise about this. Or you can alter your will later when you have had time to think about these things. The important thing is to make sure that your partner and any children are provided for if you die unexpectedly.

Guardians for children

If you have children with your partner, or from a previous relationship, you need to decide two things:

- Who do you want them to live with after your death?
- Who do you want to have responsibility for the money that you will leave them?

The answer to the first question may not be entirely within your control. If you already share parental responsibility with someone else (who is probably the children's other parent), then that person will continue to have parental responsibility after your death and would be the obvious person to have the children. However, you may be in the position of having no one you share parental responsibility with, or you may feel that another adult would be better suited to the care of your children.

If you need to, you can appoint a guardian, or guardians, in your will, or even in a simple written document (see Chapter 4). You should always check with your proposed guardians that they would be happy to take on the responsibility of your children. This may go without

---

Providing for the children's future care

Monica had two children from her marriage: Polly and Andrew. She divorced Josh, her husband, when Andrew was two, and he was not very good at keeping in contact. Two years later she met Peter and they started to live together. He had no children of his own and took a real part in looking after Polly and Andrew. They all became very close and the children saw very little of their own father, who had moved to the other end of the country and remarried. Then Monica was diagnosed with cancer and was concerned that if she died the children would have to go to Josh, rather than stay with Peter, with whom they now had a far closer bond.

She took the advice of her solicitor. She discussed her fears with Josh, who agreed that it might be better if the children stayed with Peter. She and Peter, with Josh's co-operation, got an order from the court that Peter should have parental responsibility with her and Josh. She appointed Peter the children's guardian in her will.

---

saying in the case of your partner, but you may want to think about someone else.

Trustees for your estate

Executors are the people whom you appoint to sort out the property that you leave and to make sure that your debts are paid and the property ends up in the hands of the people you wished it to go to. If you are leaving property to someone and your will says that they are not to have it immediately, you need to appoint *trustees* to look after that property until it is handed over to the beneficiary or beneficiaries. This most commonly happens with children, where they cannot inherit property in their own right until they are 18. (You may want to make sure that they do not get their hands on it until they have reached what you might feel would be a more sensible age: say, 25.) For the period until they get to the age when they are entitled to the money, someone has to look after it for them. Often, you may feel that the people you have asked to be executors might be the best people to be the trustees as well. The effect of this is that once the estate has been sorted out and most of your bequests distributed as you wished, the executors then turn into your trustees and continue to look after the property until the children grow up.

You may feel that the guardian(s) you have appointed for your children would be the best people to be the trustees of the children's money as well. But this might not necessarily be the case. Sometimes you may feel that the guardian might not be very good at managing money, or might exploit the situation. In any case, you will need two trustees for the children, and you may have only one guardian. Monica, in the case study above, appointed Peter and her best friend Emma, who was a godmother to one of the children, as her trustees. You should discuss the appointment of trustees with your solicitor.

If you don't have much (or any) money

It is easy to think that wills are only for people who have a lot of money and you do not need to bother about one if all you are going to leave is debts. However, the little you have is not going to go to your partner – even the bits and pieces that you just refer to as 'my stuff' – unless you deal with this in a will. Also, if you make a will now, and come into money (even a small amount) after you have made it, the will is still effective, and your partner will receive what you own, if this is what you have said in your will.

There is another, sadder, reason for making a will. If you die as a result of an accident and there is a claim for damages (which might be the case if the accident was caused by somebody's negligence), then the larger part of the damages is paid to your estate. It becomes part of the property that you leave. It will not go to your partner unless you have made a will; it may pass to a remote relative who happens to be your nearest blood relative (see the intestacy chart).

Not only debts

Jim and Penny had lived together for five years. They never made wills because Jim always said that he had only his debts to leave. They lived in a council flat in their joint names. Penny nursed him devotedly when he fell ill. He had variant CJD (the human disease that is thought to come from eating the meat of animals with BSE, 'mad cow disease'). After his death Penny found out that she could make a claim for damages from the government, along with the other families of people who had died from the disease. But because she was not entitled to Jim's estate, most of the damages that his estate received had to be paid to an elderly aunt, who was Jim's nearest relative. Penny received only a small amount, intended to compensate her for the care that she had given him.

Other important arrangements

There are other important arrangements that you can make as well as making a will. These will make sure that if you die, or become very ill, things will go more smoothly for your partner. Some of these are mentioned in Chapters 6 and 7. You can also provide for what you want to happen if you become incapable of looking after yourself.

Enduring power of attorney

You can sign a document called an 'enduring power of attorney', which will appoint another person to look after your affairs if you get to the point where you can no longer do this. (An ordinary power of attorney ceases to take effect if you do become incapable of managing your affairs.) You can appoint your partner as your attorney, and in this way confirm his or her status in looking after your affairs.

Generally, you would not need to do this unless you felt that your health was failing, or old age was creeping up on you. However, if your partner and your relatives do not see eye to eye you may want to make sure that your partner's status is confirmed, in case you suffer a catastrophic accident. In such a case, making an enduring power at the same time as your will may be a good idea.

You can get the appropriate form from a legal stationer's (see *Yellow Pages*) or from a solicitor. You need to make sure that it is worded carefully, so that it does not take effect immediately, but only when you can no longer manage your affairs. Take legal advice before you make a power of attorney. The charge for such a service will normally be reasonably modest.

A power of attorney gives your attorney considerable power over your finances, so you should not give it to anyone whom you do not trust absolutely. You can appoint more than one person to be your attorney, which can act as a safeguard. There is a useful website describing the effect of enduring powers of attorney and the legal position: www.publictrust.gov.uk.

If you do not make an enduring power of attorney and become incapable, then someone has to apply to the Court of Protection to get an order authorising them to be your 'receiver' and act on your behalf. The Court can grant such powers to a relative, a friend or someone in an official capacity, such as a solicitor. Your partner can apply to be your receiver. However, your relatives could oppose the application if they wished and it seems sensible to try to avoid this sort of conflict for the future. An enduring power of attorney, if expressed correctly, can take effect only once you have lost the capacity to deal with your affairs. The person whom you have appointed has to first register the power with the Court of Protection, and produce a medical certificate that confirms that you cannot look after your affairs.

Claims if you are left unprovided for

If your partner does not make a will providing for you after his or her death, you may be able to bring a claim under the Inheritance (Provision for Family and Dependants) Act 1975. You would have to show that your partner had failed to make reasonable provision for you. He or she could have done this either by leaving most or all of his or her estate to someone else, or (more likely) by not making a will at all.

If you have lived with your partner as husband and wife for a continuous period of two years, ending when he or she died, then you can claim as a cohabitant. If your period of living together is shorter than this, or was not continuous, or you were a same-sex couple, then you may still be able to claim – as a 'dependant' – if you were being maintained by your partner up to his or her death. Same-sex couples will, under the present law, count only as 'dependants'. You cannot claim in the estate of someone whom you used to live with, if he or she no longer contributes to your finances.

The court has a list of factors that it has to take into consideration in assessing your claim:

- your financial circumstances now and in the foreseeable future
- the financial circumstances of anyone who is entitled to the estate, now and in the foreseeable future
- the obligations and responsibilities that your partner had towards you or anyone entitled to the estate
- the size of the estate and what it consists of
- any physical or mental disability of you or anyone entitled to the estate
- any other matter that the court thinks relevant, including your conduct, or the conduct of anyone else involved.

Claiming as a dependant
The court must also look at the extent to which your partner had assumed responsibility for keeping you financially and the length of time that that had been the case. This means that if you have lived together for only a short time you are unlikely to get as much as you would after a long-term relationship. Similarly, you are unlikely to get much unless you can show that you were genuinely dependent. In a relationship

where you have both been earning, and you could have been self-supporting, you are unlikely to be able to make a very strong claim.

Claiming as a cohabitant

If you claim as a cohabitant you have a slightly enhanced status. The court will also take into consideration your age and the length of time that you lived with your partner before he or she died. The court also looks at the contribution that you made to the family (which can mean just the pair of you), which does not just mean financial contributions but includes looking after the home and the family. In this way you are able to argue a stronger 'moral right' to a share in the estate.

Children

If children or stepchildren are left unprovided for, you can also bring a claim for them, on the basis of their dependency. Your partner's children, if there is no will, will generally inherit the estate. If there is a will that does not provide properly for the children, however, or you have children of your own whom your partner has supported during his or her lifetime, then they have potential claims. Children of the deceased are listed as one of the categories of people who can bring a claim on the estate. If there are other children who were supported by the deceased but were not his children (or stepchildren by marriage), then they can claim as dependants. (See 'Claiming as a dependant', above.)

You might find that although you cannot be said to have been financially dependent on your partner (because of your own income or capital), you need to bring a claim on behalf of the children (whom you were both supporting), as their litigation 'next friend' – the adult who acts on their behalf.

Making a claim

You will need to take specialist legal advice on the strength of your claim and how you should go about it. There is a fairly short time limit: six months from the date of the grant of probate or administration. The grant is issued to your partner's 'personal representatives', the people who are legally entitled to sort out the estate. You or your solicitor can make sure that you get warning from the court when the grant is issued. (You are unlikely to be your partner's personal representative; it would only happen where he or she has appointed you executor of the will and left you nothing, or not enough.)

Cases of this kind are often settled in order to avoid litigation, but sometimes grief and family resentments that have festered for a long time can make things very bitter and unhappy. Litigation eats away at the amount of money in the estate, which is another reason for making a proper will.

Intestacy chart
Where will your estate go if you die without a will?

Are you married?

- **yes**
  - **Is your estate worth more than £125,000?**
    - **no** → Wife/husband gets everything.
    - **yes** → **Do you have children?**
      - **yes** → Wife/husband gets first £125,000 plus life interest in half the rest: the balance goes to the children.
      - **no** → **Do you have parents/brothers and sisters?**
        - **yes** → Wife/husband gets first £200,000 plus half the rest: the balance goes to parents, or brothers and sisters if you parents are dead.
        - **no** → Wife/husband gets everything.

- **no**
  - **Do you have children?**
    - **yes** → Shared equally between the children.*
    - **no** → **Do you have parents?**
      - **yes** → Shared equally between the parents.
      - **no** → **Do you have brothers and sisters?**
        - **yes** → Shared equally between brothers and sisters.*
        - **no** → **Do you have half brothers or sisters?**
          - **yes** → Shared equally between the half brothers and sisters.*
          - **no** → **Do you have grandparents?**
            - **yes** → Shared equally between grandparents.
            - **no** → **Do you have uncles or aunts?**
              - **yes** → Shared equally between aunts and uncles.*
              - **no** → **Do you have uncles and aunts of the half blood?†**
                - **yes** → Shared equally between half uncles and aunts.*
                - **no** → Everything goes to the Crown.

*On the statutory trusts: equally for all members of that category of people (alive or conceived) who have attained the age of 18 or married under that age and if they die before you, to their children (by bloodlines) provided they get to 18/marry.

†An uncle or aunt 'of the half blood' would be your parent's half brother or sister.

Chapter 6

Pensions and other financial matters

This chapter does not intend to be a detailed survey of pension law. *The Which? Guide to Pensions* gives you general advice about the types of pensions available and how they work. Chapter 8 in this book tells you how state benefits and state pension schemes affect you as cohabitants; you have no rights under the state scheme to benefits that depend on your partner's contributions, unless you were married to your partner.

Pensions

The detail of the way in which pension schemes work varies from scheme to scheme, but some essential features are common to them all. A pension is deferred pay: income that you postpone having until a particular event in the future, which is generally your retirement. If you die before you retire the scheme may pay out all or some of the following:

- a 'death-in-service' benefit
- a regular income to your spouse or partner for his or her life or until he or she remarries
- a regular income to your children until they get to 18.

If you reach retirement age the scheme may pay out all or some of the following:

- a lump sum (you may be able to choose the amount up to a ceiling figure)
- a regular income to you.

If you die following retirement age the scheme may pay out all or some of the following:

- a regular income to your spouse or partner for his or her life or until he or she remarries
- a regular income to your children until they get to 18.

There may also be other benefits, such as early retirement benefits or protection if you cannot work. The combinations of what you get and the proportion and size of any lump-sum payment depend on the details of the scheme.

During the time that you are paying into the pension scheme, the money that you pay in is invested in a way that is intended to create more money and let the pension fund grow. Trustees administer the scheme and they have the final decision as to how and to whom the money should be paid.

The key features, as far as this book is concerned, are the rights that your partner has in any scheme if you die first. Pensions are an area of the law where there is still considerable distinction drawn between the rights of spouses and the rights of cohabitants. And same-sex partners face even more discrimination.

Pension schemes run by your employer

If your employer runs a pension scheme this will probably be, from a financial point of view, the best way to save for your retirement. This is because your employer will contribute to the funds in the pension scheme and bear the administration costs. There are generally other benefits that are included in the scheme.

Who will get a pension payment on your death?

Not all employers' schemes will recognise an unmarried partner in the same way as they would recognise a husband or wife. You can state whom you wish to benefit in the event of your death, but the final decision remains with the trustees of the scheme. Some schemes will pay a pension after your death only to your spouse, so your partner will not receive an income from the scheme, even if you have been the sole earner in the relationship.

Can a cohabitant be a war widow?

In October 2001 there was a good deal of publicity about the situation of Anna Homsi, the bereaved partner of an SAS soldier who was killed in Sierra Leone. Had she been his widow she would have been entitled to a war widow's pension, but they had not married. After the publicity, the Ministry of Defence did agree to make a payment to her, without conceding that she had any right to it. They also offered a sum which, according to her solicitor, was about half what she would have received as a widow.

Of those schemes that will pay out a pension to your cohabitant partner, only a very small proportion will pay to a same-sex partner. About 50 per cent of the private sector and 77 per cent of the public sector schemes state that they will never pay to a same-sex partner. The law in this area may change. At the time of writing, there is a case pending in the Court of Human Rights in which Ron Strank and Roger Fisher, who have lived together for over 40 years, are taking the government to court about the absence of rights for their partners in their NHS pension. If they are successful, there should be changes in the law to recognise these rights.

Who will get your death-in-service payment?

You can nominate your death-in-service benefit so that it passes to your nominee on your death, if you die before you retire. This is tax-efficient, as it means that it does not form part of your estate on your death and cannot attract Inheritance Tax as a result; it should be paid straight to the person whom you nominated. The trustees of the scheme will normally pay out to the person or people whom you nominate. They do, however, still retain discretion about who they pay.

The sensible thing would be to check with the scheme (which you can probably do through your employer's Human Resources department). Find out what attitude the trustees will take. If they will pay to your partner, then nominate your death-in-service benefit to your partner (or in appropriate shares to your partner and your children). If you are in a same-sex relationship and you get an indication that they will not pay to a same-sex partner, then you should consider whether it might be better not to nominate the payment at all.

If you do not nominate your death-in-service benefit you are still entitled to it; instead of being paid to your nominee, it should be paid to your estate on your death. If you have left your estate, or the greater part of this, to your partner, then it will come to him or her through your will. You must make a will so that this can happen. Taking this course of action does mean, however, that the death-in-service payment forms part of your estate, and, if your estate is liable to Inheritance Tax, it will increase the tax bill. (See Chapter 9.) Take legal advice about the best course of action if you think that this would be the best thing to do. There may be a more tax-efficient option that you could take. For instance, if you have children whom you want to benefit as well as your partner, you could nominate the death-in-service benefit to them (on the basis that the trustees would almost certainly pay out to them) and leave the rest of your estate to your partner. The death-in-service benefit would not attract tax if you did this.

If your circumstances change, you can change your nomination by notifying your pension scheme. You should think about it every five years or so, just as you should review any bequests that you have made in a will, to make sure that they still suit your circumstances and take advantage of the current tax law.

Alternatives to an employer's pension scheme

If your employer's scheme does not offer satisfactory benefits for your partner, you need to decide whether to join it or not and, if you join it, whether to boost it, as far as your partner is concerned. Generally, the advice is that an employer's scheme will offer you a much better deal – for yourself – than a private pension scheme. You could consider whether you should join another private scheme that would benefit your partner, or make other savings provision through life insurance, or ISAs, PEPs or other tax-efficient savings schemes.

Your employer may also offer other schemes, such as group personal pension schemes and stakeholder schemes. These will pay a lump sum, but not a survivor's pension, if you die before reaching retirement age.

Private pension schemes

If you do not have an employer's scheme you should consider taking out a private pension scheme. There are a large number of schemes on the market and it is important to find the right one for you and your family, bearing in mind the changes that may occur during your lifetime. You will need to shop around to find a scheme that will recognise the rights of your partner (and a same-sex partner if appropriate). This may be easiest if you use the services of an independent financial adviser. Some stakeholder pensions (which are a relatively new product) are specifically intended for same-sex couples.

Life insurance

Life insurance ought to be useful for cohabitants, since it offers a way of saving and providing for a payment on your death. You can, when you buy a life insurance policy, 'write' it 'in trust', which means that you can nominate who will get the proceeds on your death. Like a nominated death-in-service benefit (as described above), a policy written in trust does not form part of your estate on your death and will go to the person whom you have named. Unlike pensions, there are no rules to life insurance that prevent you nominating the person whom you want to benefit, so life insurance gives you control over where the money will go.

However, life insurance can be a problem for cohabitants. Many companies will routinely ask single men (gay or straight) if they have had a positive HIV test. They may also send you a supplementary questionnaire which will ask you about your sexual and social history. The principal of 'utmost good faith' applies to all insurance contracts, so it is not a good idea to lie or conceal information because this gives the insurance company grounds for repudiating the policy. Most companies will also discriminate by charging higher premiums if you are gay. The higher the amount of cover, the more difficulty you are likely to find. Helpful organisations are listed at the back of this book.

Medical and health insurance

Most medical and health plans insure not only you but also (generally for a slightly increased subscription) your family. Many major providers of health and medical insurance define 'family' as including your partner, whether married or not, but do not include a same-sex partner in this definition, so same-sex partners would need to have separate cover.

Company privileges

Many companies offer their staff privileges, such as cut-price travel or discounts on merchandise, and in many cases this privilege extends to spouses. Many companies take this further and include cohabitants of the opposite or same sex. However, there is no legal requirement that they do so, and it is not illegal for companies to make a distinction between a male/female cohabiting couple and a same-sex couple.

In a case in 1998 the European Court of Justice ruled that South West Trains had not breached European equality laws when they refused to grant travel concessions to the lesbian partner of one of their female employees. The company did grant concessionary tickets to 'one common law opposite-sex spouse of staff' where there had been a meaningful relationship of at least two years. Since then the European Commission has drawn up a draft directive about discrimination in the workplace, but this has yet to be adopted by all member states, and so is not law.

Much of the law in this area seems not to be keeping pace with changing lifestyles and families. The Human Rights Act is likely to create some changes, and demand from employees will probably also mean that the law will change rapidly over the next few years.

Chapter 7

Being treated as the next of kin

One of the things that worries cohabitants is being recognised as each other's 'next of kin'. Throughout this book situations are highlighted in which you are or are not treated as being 'related' as far as the law is concerned. This chapter deals with the issues surrounding medical treatment and personal injury.

Medical treatment

Many people worry about how their partners will be treated if they have to go into hospital. Will the hospital recognise the position of your partner if a treatment decision needs to be made? Will they explain treatment to him or her, will they consult with him or her? The fear is that the hospital could be excessively legalistic and treat your partner as having no valid relationship with you.

In fact, most medical practitioners and hospitals will be sensitive to the issue and will understand that your partner is the person closest to you. They will realise that you would want your partner to be involved in any decision that you are unable to take for yourself. A same-sex couple may have a little more difficulty, but if you put your partner's name on any form where you are asked to state your next of kin the hospital should not try to be excessively technical about this, and should respect your wishes.

Consent to medical treatment

You may worry about what will happen if you cannot consent to treatment for yourself: will your partner be asked to consent on your behalf, or would the hospital have to locate your nearest blood relative, to ask him or her? In fact, consent to treatment does not work like this. If you are capable of giving consent to a medical procedure, the doctors will ask you. If you cannot give your consent, because you are too ill, mentally or physically, then the law says that nobody can give consent on your behalf. Instead the doctors have to give you treatment according to reasonable clinical practice and having regard to what would be in your best interests. The guidelines from the Department of Health say that: 'It is good practice for the healthcare team to involve those close to the patient in order to find out about the patient's values and preferences before loss of capacity, unless the patient has previously made clear that particular individuals should not be involved.' This would normally be in the situation where you are unable to make decisions for yourself over some considerable period of time – perhaps if you were being supported on a ventilator in an intensive care unit. If you are only temporarily incapacitated – briefly unconscious after an accident, for instance – then you can be given whatever treatment is necessary and regarded by those treating you as being in your best interests.

If there is doubt about what would be in your best interests (which generally means whatever treatment represents the least risk to you as the patient), the doctors can apply to the court for a ruling. This would happen only in very unusual circumstances. The Department of Health guidelines clearly do not exclude cohabitants from being consulted about your treatment wishes, and assume the possibility that you could state, in advance, that you did not want other people to be consulted. For the avoidance of doubt, you could write this on an organ donor card. (Some people write other wishes on these cards, such as a refusal to be visited by the Prime Minister or any member of the Royal Family in the event of a disaster!) You could also make a 'living will': an advance directive of the sort of treatment that you would want to have.

Living wills

'Living wills' (which are sometimes also called 'advance directives') may sound like legal documents, but they are not. They are statements of your wishes about the sort of treatment and care that you would want if you became incurably ill. You can say whether you would want to be kept alive by all means, or what treatment you would want to refuse. You can state in such a document whom you want the doctors to consult, and make it clear that your partner should be asked for his or her consent to treatment for you if you cannot give your own consent. Doctors have a duty always to treat according to what is in the best interests of the patient, so your living will could not compel them to a course of treatment, but would probably be persuasive if there was a choice of treatments to be applied.

Organ donation

Again, the position about organ donation is not generally understood very clearly. If you die and you have given your consent in advance by signing an organ donation card, the hospital may take your organs for medical treatment. Your family do not have to be consulted, legally, but generally are, as a matter of medical courtesy. Most hospitals will discuss it with whoever has been closest to the patient. Sometimes conflicts may arise between partners and parents, especially if they have never got on during your lifetime. Hospitals do not generally want to go against the wishes of your family, even if you have completed a donor card. The advice on the organ donor website (www.nhsorgan-donor.net) is that you should discuss your decision with your family and let them know what you intend to do.

If you do not carry an organ donor card, then the decision has to be made by your family in discussion with the hospital. This could produce a bitter and unhappy situation, if your partner is saying one thing and your parents another. Spare everyone the anguish by making your wishes clear one way or another. A donor card would confirm your wish to donate. A statement in your will could confirm that you did or did not wish parts of your body to be removed – but you should tell those closest to you as well.

Personal injury rights

The area of law that deals with compensation for injury is a complex one, and you should take specialist legal advice about your position if your partner is injured or killed. What follows is a brief outline of the law in this area to give you an indication of what your position may be. The term 'accident', under the Fatal Accidents Act 1976, means any negligent event that causes your death, which could be one event or a gradual injury such as asbestosis.

Generally speaking, if you sustain an injury during your life that gives rise to a right to be compensated, then your cohabiting partner (but not necessarily a same-sex partner) is treated in much the same way as a spouse and little material distinction is drawn. For that reason, this section covers only injury that leads to death. The situation is different for death: where one partner (who has not left a will) is killed in circumstances that give rise to a claim for damages. The bereaved partner may have to rely entirely on the goodwill of blood relatives in order to get what would be his or her 'rightful' share of the damages.

In a claim that arises from the death of one partner, the overall damages are broken down under different headings which establish different entitlements. These are set out below: you will see that there is no automatic way in which your partner will receive the total of any sums that might be paid in damages for your death. Some will come to him or her, but others will go into your estate (the money that you leave behind on your death).

Pain, suffering and loss of amenity

This is also referred to as 'general damages'. It is a sum paid to compensate the experience of the person who has died, in the circumstances that led to his or her death. This is money to compensate for the pain and suffering that you underwent. Although in one sense money cannot make up for the pain, there is a recognised legal tariff for different types of injury. If a person dies almost immediately from a road accident, his or her estate will receive less than it would if the person had had a long and painful period of suffering, for example from exposure to asbestos during employment.

The claim for these damages is brought by the dead person's estate – that is, by his or her personal representatives. These would be your executors if you had left a will, or your next of kin (as shown on the intestacy chart in Chapter 5) if you die intestate (without a will). The money is paid into your estate, so it goes to the beneficiaries of your will, or, if you die intestate, to your next of kin.

Direct financial losses

Another portion of damages compensates for the actual financial losses that you suffer as a result of death; this replaces lost earnings and other financial benefits that you might have lost as a result of your death. You may feel that this is immaterial, since you are not going to have the benefit of it, but this money is added to your estate so that you do not die poorer as a result of an accident. Again, this is a claim brought by your estate, and paid into your estate.

Bereavement damages

This is a sum fixed by the Fatal Accidents Act 1976. Currently it is £7,500 and can be paid only to a bereaved spouse. Although cohabitants can bring claims under other sections of the Act, they are not entitled to this payment.

Past and future economic losses and dependency claims for partners

If your partner has suffered a loss because of your accident – for instance, because he or she has had to give up work to nurse you through a last illness – he or she can bring a claim on his or her own behalf to compensate for this loss.

In addition, under the Fatal Accidents Act 1976 a dependant can bring a claim based on the fact that she or he has lost financial support as a result of your death. The Act defines a dependant as including a spouse (or former spouse) and also a cohabitant: if you have been living with the deceased, as husband and wife, for a continuous period of two years immediately before the date of death. (If you have been living together for a shorter time you are not eligible to make a claim.) Same-sex partners are not eligible to make a claim under this Act, although there is likely to be a challenge to this under the Human Rights Act in the near future. (Just being a financial dependant does not bring you within the scope of the Act.)

The damages for loss of dependency are worked out using a method of calculation based on the notional life expectancy (had the accident not occurred) of the person who has died.

These damages are paid to the person who has suffered the loss: they do not go into your estate.

Dependency claims for children

Your children, too, can bring claims for loss of dependency, to cover the years from the date of the accident until they get to 18, or, if the court decides that they are likely to go on to further education, until they are 21. 'Children' can include your stepchildren, even if you are not married – though this is not the case in other statutes such as the Inheritance (Provision for Family and Dependants) Act 1976 (see Chapter 5).

If damages are paid for children, these are held in the court and your partner can draw on them only with specific permission of the court and for particular expenses for the children, such as school uniform.

Chapter 8

State benefits

This chapter is not intended as a detailed account of the state benefit system, but to highlight how cohabiting couples fit into the benefits system. The Department of Work and Pensions* maintains an extremely helpful website, from which its leaflets can be downloaded, and very effective telephone helplines. Also, the Child Poverty Action Group* publishes a very good guide to the benefits system.

State benefits that work on a means-tested basis deal with families as units whether they are married or not, and there is little distinction made between a couple living together and a married couple. This has been the case for a remarkably long time. The 1966 social security legislation recognised that a cohabiting couple were to be treated as if they were married. However, this does not apply to a same-sex couple; there is no state benefit where the reference to 'your partner' in the regulations can mean someone of the same sex. It seems inevitable that this will change. The 1966 change was not inspired by liberal enlightenment on the part of the government, but because otherwise more would have to be paid in benefits, as cohabiting families would have been able to make two claims. This is the case now with same-sex couples, who can, where financial circumstances allow it, each make a claim for benefit. As the number of same-sex couples grows, the government will surely decide that this 'loop-hole' must be dealt with, and decree that a same-sex couple must be treated as a single family.

Benefits that depend on contributions that you have paid in, such as state pension or widow(er)'s benefit, do make a distinction between married and cohabiting couples. They are paid only if your spouse, not your cohabitant, has made the correct National Insurance contributions.

Child benefit

Child benefit can be claimed by anyone who has a child living with him or her, and the child does not have to be the child of the person who claims. It is paid to only one adult in a couple – generally, but not necessarily, the mother. Only one amount of child benefit for each child is paid each week, so two people cannot claim for the same child simultaneously. If one of you is not working you can get state retirement pension protection if you are claiming child benefit, on the basis that you are not working because you are looking after children. It makes sense, if one of you is not working, for the non-worker to claim the child benefit.

If you and your partner both bring children from a previous relationship to the family, you can have only one child classed as the eldest child (receiving the higher rate of benefit: £15.75 as opposed to £10.55 in 2002–3). However, same-sex couples in this situation can both claim for their eldest child.

Income support or jobseeker's allowance

Income support or jobseeker's allowance (you get one or the other, depending on your circumstances) is paid on a family-unit basis, so you get it only if you and your partner's financial circumstances, and also the numbers of hours that you both work, qualify you for it. You can get income support only if you do not have to sign on at a job centre. You have to be working fewer than 16 hours a week, and your partner fewer than 24 hours a week.

If you and your partner are both seeking work you will have to make a joint claim for jobseeker's allowance.

As this does not apply to same-sex couples, you can make individual claims based on your individual circumstances.

Working families' tax credit

Working families' tax credit is a top-up payment paid through the Inland Revenue, so that you get the benefit of it in your pay packet. It can also include the cost of childcare. You can claim it if you have at least one child and you or your partner work 16 hours or more a week. (You cannot add your hours together to make up a total of 16.) You have to have no more than £8,000 in capital. If one of you works more than 30 hours a week there is an additional payment.

The credit is assessed and paid on a six-monthly basis, so once an award is made it will run for six months, even if your circumstances change during that time. It is a very helpful benefit, increasing the income of your family significantly. Payments of child maintenance are not counted in the assessment of the amount that you should receive. Again, a same-sex couple could, if their individual circumstances merited it, make a claim each.

Widowed parent's allowance and other benefits for widow(er)s

If your husband or wife has died and you are bringing up children, or you are a widow expecting your former husband's baby, you can claim this benefit. It continues while your children are at school. However, your entitlement ends if you remarry or cohabit. You would be able to claim it, therefore, only if you are now living in a same-sex relationship, so it is included for completeness in this section of the book.

Your former spouse had to have been paying National Insurance contributions and it does only apply to widows and widowers – that is, you must have been married at the time of the death to the person who has died, not just have been living with him or her. The amount in 2000–1 is £67.50 a week, which is the basic payment. Other benefits may affect the amount that you get. Widows and widowers are also entitled to a one-off sum of £2,000 on the death of their spouse, provided the spouse made National Insurance contributions, or died as a result of his or her job. Your spouse, or you yourself, also have to be below state pension age at the time of the death. (The current state pension age for women is 60. However, women will be brought into line with men for a standard retirement age of 65 by the year 2020.)

Pension

You are not entitled to a state pension on the death of your cohabitant. The National Insurance contributions that a person makes during his or her lifetime can only benefit the person or his or her spouse.

Chapter 9

Tax

As far as the Inland Revenue is concerned, you are either married or single; there is no 'halfway house'. You might be two complete strangers, from their point of view. There is nothing that you can do about this: you are disadvantaged compared with a married couple in some respects, notably in Inheritance Tax law, but in Capital Gains Tax you may be able to take limited advantage of being treated as two single people.

Income tax

The differences between married and unmarried couples are fewer than they were. The married couple's allowance ceased to operate from 5th April 2000, except for elderly spouses, where one or other of the couple is over 65. Each adult in a couple is entitled to a personal allowance and is taxed separately.

Children's tax credit

The children's tax credit, which started on 6 April 2001, is not dependent on married status. It is paid if you have a child living with you who is under 16 and is your own child or one whom you look after at your own expense. It reduces the amount of income tax that you have to pay, up to a maximum reduction of £442 (in 2001–2).

You can have one tax credit for each family. 'Family' in this context includes an unmarried family, but not a same-sex couple with children. A same-sex couple have the slightly advantageous position of each being able to claim for a child, provided they do not both claim for the same child.

You can have the tax credit only if you are a tax payer. Higher-rate tax payers get a reduced amount, on a sliding scale. If your income is over about £41,000 you are unlikely to receive any benefit. A couple can choose who is to get the credit, or whether they will share it. If one of you is a higher-rate payer and the other isn't, then the lower earner should claim the credit. If you do not pay enough tax to use up all the credit, you can transfer the unused credit to your partner at the end of the tax year. If you are both higher-rate payers, the partner with the higher income must claim the credit and you cannot share it or transfer it between you.

If you start or stop living with your partner during the tax year, you should tell the Inland Revenue. The tax credit is then apportioned over the year.

If your child or children live with someone else as well as you for part of the year, the tax credit can be divided between you. This would happen where, for instance, you had been married and your children from this marriage spent the week with you and the weekends with your ex-spouse. If you cannot agree the shares in which the credit should be divided, the Inland Revenue commissioners can make a decision for you. If you have more than one child and the children spend more than 30 days a year with one parent (as they would if they spend alternate weekends with their father, say), then you may each be able to claim a full tax credit. The tax office will be able to advise you on this.

Inheritance Tax

This section of the book is not intended to be an exhaustive description of the way in which the tax system can affect you. But since Inheritance Tax (IHT) is not widely understood, and generally affects you only on death, here is a quick guide to the essential points.

Inheritance Tax is charged on the value of your estate when you die. It is charged in two bands. The first band of your estate (£242,000 in 2001–2) is charged at nil per cent (this is referred to as the 'nil rate band') and anything above this at 40 per cent. For Inheritance Tax purposes, your estate includes the half-share of anything that you owned jointly, as well as all the property in your sole name. It also includes the value of any gifts that you have made over the last seven calendar years before your death. Your debts at the date of your death and your funeral expenses can be deducted from this total.

Your estate (again, for Inheritance Tax purposes) does not include the value of any life insurance policy that you have assigned or 'written in trust' for someone else. Nor does it include a death-in-service payment, if, during your lifetime, you have nominated who is to have this. These are treated as being the beneficiary's property and not yours, so they do not fall into your estate.

Inheritance Tax can also be charged during your lifetime. In any seven-year period of your lifetime you can give away up to the nil rate band for the time being. If you give away more than this, the gifts can be charged to Inheritance Tax, which the person who gets the gift is liable to pay. If you have the sort of money which allows you to make gifts and settlements at this level, you should be aware of the tax implications and should take proper and detailed legal advice about the best way of structuring such gifts.

Transfers between husbands and wives are exempt for Inheritance Tax purposes, so any money left by a husband to his wife and vice versa will not attract tax. Cohabitants have no such concession. If your estate is likely to be more than the nil rate band (and the value of your home in times of rising house prices can make up a hefty proportion of this), then you should take some legal advice about the best way of dealing with your assets.

Some of the techniques that you could consider would include:

- equalising your estates during your lifetimes
- buying life insurance for each other
- buying a life insurance policy to cover the expected IHT bill
- 'nominating' any lump-sum payment in your pension scheme (but see Chapter 6 about possible difficulties with this).

The younger you are when you buy insurance policies, the cheaper they are likely to be.

Capital Gains Tax

To describe it simply, Capital Gains Tax (CGT) is charged on the profit made when an asset is disposed of (or charged on the increase in value since it was acquired). A 'disposal' can be a sale or a gift. Each individual has an annual exemption for gains (£7,500 in 2001–2), and there are allowances for inflation. Assets which are 'wasting assets', that is, whose value goes down from year to year, are exempt, so selling your car will not attract CGT. You are also allowed an exemption for the sale of your 'principal private residence'. A husband and wife are generally allowed only one principal private residence between them.

If you have two homes, as cohabitants you actually have the advantage of each being able to nominate one of the properties as your 'principal private residence'. You have to be able to show to the Inland Revenue that you have spent a substantial amount of time in the property. If you had simply owned it for the purpose of renting it out, for instance, the exemption would not apply.

'Disposals' or transfers between husband and wife are free of CGT. There is no similar rule for cohabitants. However, CGT will not impinge on your life much unless you are making large gifts between each other. If you plan to do this, as with IHT, you need to take legal and/or financial advice about the best way of doing it.

Chapter 10

What changes if you marry

This chapter is a summary of the changes in your legal position that take place if you marry. Much of it you may have already been able to work out from the comparisons with married couples that are included in the rest of the book. Many couples not only live in ignorance of their legal positions when they are living together, but also have only a hazy notion of the legal implications of marriage, if they do tie the knot. This chapter is included to clarify the situation. The table 'Differences in the legal treatment of married and cohabiting couples' at the beginning of the book also highlights the differences in each area of the law.

There has been a great deal of publicity about the introduction of a register for cohabitants in London. Other cities plan to do the same thing. In the UK, so far it is mainly same-sex couples, who want to declare their relationship as a 'marriage', who have taken up the opportunity to register. A number of European states have introduced ways in which cohabitants can register their relationship and, as a result, affect their legal status. It is important to remember that if you are a cohabiting couple in the UK and you register your relationship, you are not, under the law as it stands, able to change the legal nature of your relationship. If the law should changes you would have to make sure that you are prepared to accept all the legal consequences of a registered relationship. A registered relationship may be given exactly the same status as a heterosexual marriage, or there may be statutory limits; at the time of writing it is impossible to predict what the consequences will be.

Changes when you marry
Names

Contrary to popular belief, there is no requirement for the wife to take her husband's surname on marriage. Her use of his name is a courtesy title. If you wish to change your name you can do so, but it is your choice. You may encounter an occasional raised eyebrow if you keep your 'maiden' name, but it is becoming more and more common for women not to change their names. If you want to change your name, all you have to do is produce your marriage certificate and organisations such as banks will alter their records. English law is very informal in its requirements for change of name and you do not have to have an official document of any sort. You do not need a deed poll, or a statutory declaration of change of name, when you marry. Nor do you need one if you decide to change your name for any other reason; it is enough, in law, if you simply change your name and tell everyone who needs to know. This does not stop banks and some other organisations trying to insist that you produce an official document such as a deed poll as formal confirmation of your decision.

Name changing: it's your choice

Alice, a solicitor, married her boyfriend Kevin, with whom she had been living. They had had a joint bank account before their marriage, which showed their two (different) surnames. Alice decided, for professional reasons, that she would not take Kevin's name. They wrote to their bank to tell the manager that they were married and received back a rather stroppy letter ordering them to send in their marriage certificate so that the names on their account could be changed. Alice had to write back to the bank to inform them that she did not intend to change her name. She was also fairly offended that the bank did not seem prepared to take her word that she had married and wanted her to supply proof.

If you have had children before you marry, and you want to change their surname, you can also simply do this by telling people. If you want to mark the occasion in a formal, official way you can, as a parent, execute a deed poll on each child's behalf which will formally record the change of name.

Children can be very upset by their surname being altered, so you should consult their wishes in this rather than taking a decision without asking them.

The law is different if you have children from a previous marriage who are your partner's stepchildren and you want them to change to his surname on your marriage. The courts have recently made it clear that you should not make a decision on your own to change your children's surnames; you should try to get the consent of their father (assuming that they have his surname) and, failing that, you should make an application to the court. Courts are generally reluctant to sanction children

---

Passport Office requirements if you change a child's name

You will need to prove the name change if you apply for a passport for a child who is known by a different name from that on the birth certificate. You can do this with:

- a 'change of name' deed, witnessed by a solicitor or commissioner for oaths
- a statutory declaration setting out the change of name, made before a solicitor or commissioner for oaths
- a letter from an older relative, or other responsible person such as your doctor or minister of religion, who has known your child with both names and can testify that the change of name has been made for all purposes.

---

losing their father's name, unless you can show that it would be in their best interests to do so.

Inheritance

If you marry, you each become the other's next of kin as far as inheritance is concerned. However, if you have already made a will your marriage will revoke it automatically. (Wilkie Collins' novel *No Name*, published in 1862, hinges on this legal point.) This means that immediately after your marriage you will be intestate: have no valid will. You may feel that this is not a problem because, as you can see from the intestacy chart at the end of Chapter 5, your husband or wife will now inherit a substantial chunk of your estate. But the statutory amount is not enormous: £125,000 if you have children and £200,000 if you are childless, but have parents or brothers and sisters alive. Also, you will lose any provision in your will for children, or about guardians.

You can avoid this problem by making a will before you marry 'in contemplation of marriage', so that it will not be revoked on your marriage. As it is almost impossible to rush into marriage at a moment's notice, you should arrange to make a new will as soon as you decide that you are going to marry, and in this way solve the potential legal problem. A solicitor can draw up a will for you that becomes effective only if and when you marry. This means that if you have an existing will it continues to have effect until your marriage, and then the new one takes over. This solves the problem of a temporary intestacy. Both of you should make wills like this. It also gives you a chance to revisit the arrangements that you have made and think, for instance, about stepchildren, or other relatives that you may acquire by marriage.

Parental responsibility

If you have children with your partner and have not shared parental responsibility for them before now, their father will automatically acquire parental responsibility on your marriage. In Chapter 4 we describe what this entails. It means that you will both have full parental status. It would be sensible, therefore, to tell the children's schools and your doctor that you have married, even though you may not want to make a big issue of it. It makes no difference to your children's inheritance rights or to payment of child support, however, as the law already makes no distinction between children of married and unmarried parents.

Stepchildren: children of the family

If your partner has children whom you treat as children of the family after your marriage, the law treats you as having assumed a financial responsibility for them. If you subsequently divorce, your husband or wife could bring a claim for their maintenance in the divorce proceedings. She or he could not, however, use the Child Support Agency, as this deals only with children who are yours by birth or adoption. Children who have been treated as children of the family can also make claims under the Inheritance (Provision for Family and Dependants) Act 1975, which is described in Chapter 4.

Tax

Chapter 9 outlines the considerable differences in the tax treatment of unmarried and married couples. Once you are married you can have the Inheritance Tax and Capital Gains Tax exemptions. You lose, however, the potential to have two principal private residences. Marriage will not affect your income tax position unless one or both of you are pensioners.

Pension

You automatically become each other's next of kin for pension purposes. If either of you dies, the survivor will be the widow or widower and be entitled to all the benefits under the other's pension scheme that are provided for a widow or widower. You should therefore inform the company that administers your pension scheme, or your employer (for an occupational pension scheme), that you have married.

Marriage can preserve a pension

Alan and Helen had lived together for many years without getting married. 'We never got round to it somehow, and after a while it didn't bother us.' Alan was the breadwinner and had a good salary and pension package from his employers, for whom he had worked all his life. About a year before he retired he began to have health problems and started to worry about what would happen to Helen if he died before she did.

'I went to see my solicitor. I had made a will years ago, but I knew that the company pension scheme would not pay out to a partner if you were not married. I didn't see why all the money that I had paid in over the years should go to waste if I died first. I decided that it would be best if we did get married and I went home and proposed. We had a quiet ceremony and ran off to Venice for a honeymoon. I felt so much better knowing that Helen would be provided for.'

State benefits

Most state benefits, as described in Chapter 8, make no distinction between the married and unmarried family; but there is a difference when it comes to those benefits which are dependent on payments of National Insurance contributions: state pension and widow(er)'s benefit. Once married you will become eligible for these.

If the relationship ends

What happens if we split up?

If you split up after you marry, then all the law that deals with divorce applies to you. The courts have wide powers to order maintenance between spouses and adjust ownership of property. Any property (including pension policies) that either party owns is treated as a matrimonial asset which the court can redistribute, though it will not necessarily do so. This is a considerable change from your position as cohabitants: there is no power to order maintenance between former cohabitants for each other (only for the children); and, as Chapter 13 sets out, the powers of the court to deal with property are limited to establishing what shares joint assets are held in, rather than ordering transfers of one person's assets to the other.

The result of this is that a married woman will almost certainly get more than a cohabiting woman if the relationship breaks up. The classic example of this is Mick Jagger and Jerry Hall. Because their 'marriage' was not recognised in English law, she came away from the relationship with far less than she would have received if they had been recognised as legally married (though most of us might feel that a £7 million settlement with a £5 million house would enable us to manage).

Wives are probably getting larger settlements since the case of *White v White*, in October 2000, in which a husband and wife who had been farmers in partnership with each other fought their financial settlement all the way to the House of Lords. This caused a shift in the way in which the divorce courts look at the entitlement of husband and wife. The House of Lords said that courts should use the 'yardstick of equality' in their approach to the distribution of assets in a marriage. This does not mean that in every case there will be an even split, but the tendency will be to look towards that. The ripples from this decision have yet to settle down so that lawyers can confidently predict how assets will be distributed in every case, but the broad consensus seems to be that in most cases where there are substantial assets wives will tend to receive bigger settlements than they might have expected, say, five years ago.

Financial orders on divorce

The factors that the court has to take into consideration in deciding whether to make financial orders on divorce, and what orders it should make, are:

- the income, earning capacity, property and other financial resources of both spouses, both now and in the foreseeable future, including any increased earning capacity which the court could reasonably expect either person to try to acquire
- the financial needs, obligations and responsibilities of both spouses, both now and in the foreseeable future
- the standard of living before the breakdown of the marriage
- the ages of both spouses
- the length of the marriage
- any physical or mental disabilities
- the contributions of each spouse to the welfare of the family, including any contribution in caring for the family or looking after the home, both in the past and in the foreseeable future
- in some circumstances, the conduct of either spouse
- the value of any benefit, such as a pension, which either spouse would lose the chance of acquiring as a result of the divorce.

Are the years of cohabitation taken into account?

There is an unhappy statistic that marriages that follow periods of cohabitation tend to last for a shorter time than those where the parties did not cohabit beforehand. If you divorce, you can see from the list in the box that the court takes the length of your marriage into consideration. At one time the court would not give weight to any period during which you lived together before marriage. In cases where the parties had lived together for many years before what was, comparatively, a short marriage, the attitude of the court seemed unfair, though strictly speaking it was carrying out the statute. However, the court can take length of cohabitation into account as being one of the circumstances of the case, especially if circumstances prevented you from marrying, and that was why you were cohabiting.

What if we were engaged?

If you are engaged and cohabiting and you then split up, the courts have rather more powers to make financial orders for both of you. These come (oddly, it may seem) from the Married Women's Property Act 1882, which was the first Act that recognised a married woman's power to own property in her own right. This was later extended in scope to include engaged couples, and you can apply to the court within three years of the termination of the agreement to marry.

The court can deal with all forms of property, from real property (houses and land) to household contents and bank accounts. The court can declare who owns what and can also order property to be sold. The principles (trust principles) that the court uses in deciding who owns what are as described in Chapter 15. There may be direct evidence about who paid for things, or the court may have to use trust principles to work out who ought to own the property. The court does not have powers under this Act to order maintenance, however.

Part III

Breaking up

Breaking up can be worse for cohabiting couples than it is for married couples. This is because there is no recognised process that you can go through to unscramble your relationship; divorce may be painful, but at least it offers a structure for sorting everything out. You may also have the subtle problem that people are less sympathetic, taking the attitude that it was bound to break up because you did not marry in the first place. This can be extraordinarily hurtful, because it treats your relationship as if it were second-class, and as though you are not entitled to grieve.

It may also seem as though there is nowhere to turn for help. There are a number of services that offer help and counselling for people whose marriages break up, and it may not be immediately apparent that they will (for the most part) also offer the same help to a cohabiting couple who are in difficulties. Relate,* which most people still remember as Marriage Guidance, will help a cohabiting couple and so will mediation services (see Chapter 11). Family lawyers, who deal mostly with divorce, will also be able to help you. The best way to find a helpful family solicitor is to contact the Solicitors Family Law Association,* or the Law Society.* Since different areas of law do apply to you as a cohabitant, it would be sensible to find out in your first telephone call to the firm whether they have a lawyer who has experience of dealing with cohabitants' problems.

The other problem that some cohabitants face is that because there is no legal process like divorce that allows all the issues to be looked at, the matters that you need to resolve can drag on for an unbearable length of time. This is partly because of one's natural tendency to put off dealing with unpleasant issues. But legal disputes tend to become more and more difficult to resolve the longer they are left. This is partly because it is harder to gather evidence about what really happened as memories fade, and partly because the longer things are left the more entrenched people's positions become, so getting to a settlement is harder. If you think that you are going to need to sort things out with lawyers, or in court, try to take action sooner rather than later, but always with the objective of reaching an amicable settlement, if you can.

Chapter 11
Mediation

Mediation has, in the last twenty or so years, become an accepted way of resolving all sorts of differences, whether legal or not. Lawyers at first treated it with suspicion, if only because it appeared to be taking away their livelihoods, but many lawyers now, particularly those working in the field of family law, would recommend their clients to use a mediation service to try to resolve their difficulties if possible.

'Mediation' used to be used interchangeably with the term 'conciliation' and consequently, because of the closeness of the term 'reconciliation', gave the impression that the aim was to try to get you back together again. But this is not what it sets out to do. A mediator tries to help both of you reach your own solution about what is best and fair. The process involves allowing both of you to have your say, about your feelings and about the practical needs that both of you have.

The value of the process is in this twofold nature. You cannot separate people's problems from their feelings about them, but sometimes it can feel as though the law ignores the emotional side of the problem. Both aspects need to be worked through in order for you to come to terms with the changes that are happening in your life. For this reason mediation is a 'good thing'.

Mediation also has a particular advantage for cohabitants. This is because the alternative – a fight via lawyers and in court – is more complicated and potentially expensive than it would be for a married couple. Mediation is a form of negotiation, one that seeks to achieve a 'win/win' solution; that is, a solution where both parties come away with something that they wanted. In all forms of negotiation, you have to be aware of what the alternative is if the negotiation fails. For cohabitants this can be protracted litigation in a field where the outcomes are by no means as clear-cut as they are for divorcing couples. Since you have – potentially – more to lose by litigating, you have more to gain – potentially – by mediating.

Another aspect of mediation that makes it particularly valuable for families, whether the parents are married or not, is that all-or-nothing negotiation, of the kind where you hope to beat your opponent and gain the upper hand, is fundamentally damaging to a continuing relationship. Where you have children, you may cease to be partners, but you will never be able to end being parents. Somehow, out of the pain and chaos, you have to find a way of continuing to have a civilised relationship, because of the children. Mediation, with its emphasis on a win/win solution, makes it easier to continue to have a relationship. It can even teach you a new way of communicating that you can build on for the future.

Mediation services can help to sort out issues about your children, or money, or deal with both these aspects of your lives, if you need them to.

The process

The style of mediation will vary from service to service, but in general what you will be offered is a series of appointments for you to attend as a couple. The typical pattern would be five or six meetings. These will be run by a mediator or a pair of mediators. Some services will have solicitor mediators, who will work in tandem with other mediators whose backgrounds may be in social work, or related fields such as probation or counselling. If you are going to try to sort out your financial arrangements, you will both be asked to disclose your complete financial position to the mediator(s) and to each other. You will be given a ques-tionnaire-type form on which you can set this out. The principle of 'full and frank disclosure' comes from divorce law and is equally relevant to cohabitants. The idea is that you should not ask someone to come to an agreement in ignorance of the other person's position; a court has powers to compel disclosure if it is not volunteered.

Once you both know about each other's financial position, you can each put forward what you think would be the best way of settling things between you. You may have a range of options and the mediator may suggest others. Generally the mediator will write these up on a flip-chart or board so that you can consider and modify them.

All meetings with mediators are 'legally privileged' (sometimes referred to as 'without prejudice'): this means that what is said in them is private to those meetings, and what you say cannot be quoted against you in court. The only significant exception to the privilege rule would be if it became apparent that someone, particularly a child, is suffering or likely to suffer 'significant harm'. The mediator in such circum-stances might feel that the mediation would have to stop and he or she would have to take steps to protect the child.

If you manage to reach an agreement, it is not binding upon you or your partner until you have both had a chance to take it to your solicitors and/or have it drawn up in a legally binding form. Normally the mediator will write out the agreement, setting out first the details of financial disclosure on which the agreement has been based. You and your partner will be asked to sign the agreement to show that you confirm the contents. The details about your financial positions will be 'open' – they could be disclosed to a court, because the court has to have this information before an order can be made – but the agreement will remain 'without prejudice' until it has been cast into a legal form such as a deed or a court order. Mediators will be careful to give you the space and time to air your feelings, as well as to discuss the practical arrangements that you need to make. After getting you to acknowledge your feelings, they will also try to get you to move on from there to focus on the future. Sometimes the legacy of your relationship may be a good deal of emotional turmoil for one or other of you. Mediation cannot generally deal with this – it is not counselling, or therapy, though mediators will have some of those skills – and a mediator may suggest that you or your partner may also need help of this kind.

It can be difficult (particularly if you are someone who works in similar fields to mediation) to submit yourself to the process. It is all too easy to be conscious of the technique that the mediator is bringing to bear on the meeting, and the way in which you are being 'managed'. This can make you resentful and resistant to the process, even though you have chosen to use it in the first place. Perhaps here we all need a little humility. It is never easy to accept that our lives have become messed up, especially if we feel that we might be somehow responsible. This in itself can make it hard to deal with the process of getting things straight again. But if you 'go along' with the process that is proposed and try to put your judgements and prejudices aside, you will get more out of it and it will be a more productive experience for you and your partner.

Finding a mediation service

You can look in *Yellow Pages* under 'Mediation'; or your local county court's family section should generally be able to tell you if there is a local service. The Citizens Advice Bureau will also usually be able to tell you about your nearest service. Most services will be affiliated to National Family Mediation★ and their central office (www.nfm.u-net.com) has a directory of local services. Local family solicitors should be able to recommend you to a service. Quite a few solicitors now offer a mediation service themselves. The Solicitors Family Law Association* keeps a list of lawyer mediators as well.

The mediation service will tell you the cost of each session. Each partner in a couple will be billed separately, and there may be concessionary rates, depending on your financial position. Lawyer mediators will probably charge more than charitable mediation services. It used to be said that it was cheaper to go to mediation than to lawyers; this is not necessarily the case, but it will generally be cheaper than having a full-blown fight in court.

If you are eligible for public funding, which is what Legal Aid is now called, you may arrive at mediation by a different route. If you have a legal dispute with your partner and need public funding, you will automatically be sent to a mediation service to see whether mediation can help resolve your difficulties. The Community Legal Service* pays for the mediation. As well as having particular advantages for cohabitants, the other considerable advantage is that the Statutory Charge (which is the way the Legal Services Commission gets you to pay back what it has paid out in costs) does not apply to agreements that you reach via mediation. This is designed as a deliberate incentive to encourage people to use mediation as a way of resolving disputes.

Chapter 12

Arrangements for the children

If you are splitting up and you have children, you obviously need to give a good deal of thought to what would be the best arrangements for them in the future. Cohabitations are statistically more fragile than marriages, and some or all of your children may already have been through one separation and be even more vulnerable to a new disruption. If you approach the split thoughtfully, and communicate sensibly with the children, as well as trying to be as amicable with each other as you can manage, you will lessen the hurt that the split may cause them.

This chapter is intended to give you some general pointers about sensible ways of handling the situation. There are a number of good books on the market about family break-up and how you deal with the children, as well as organisations to help you, many of which are listed at the back of this book.

It is important to acknowledge that you are not going to be at your best as parents while the separation is happening. You are going to be unhappy and stressed and this will make it difficult for you to be rational and even-tempered. You will probably feel at times that you need to be looked after as though you were a child. This may make you feel very guilty and will make it hard for you to be the good parent you would like to be. Try to take comfort from the fact that this is a temporary state. Things will change, though it may take some time, and by next year life will be different and probably better. You have to get through a bad stage as a family, each looking after the others. However much you now dislike (or even hate) your partner, remember the key fact that you are both going to go on being parents for the rest of your lives. Your children will still need you there for their weddings, births, illnesses, crises. Think about whether you want to continue in a state of armed truce every time you meet; whether you want your children to feel they can never invite you to the same occasion; whether you want to continue to hate each other for the rest of your lives. Somehow you need to find a way of coping with each other in the future.

Many couples, probably most, manage to find a way of doing this. For some it takes quite a while. If you do not find a way, the people that you hurt will be your children. However badly you yourselves are hurting, it is not fair to drag them into the quarrel.

Telling the children

All the available advice on this matter is that, if possible, you should tell them together and you should do it in such a way that they can ask questions and talk and be hugged and reassured. This may be impossible: if your partner has left without much warning and you remain with the children, you will be faced with their questions and may not be able to arrange to answer these as a couple. Try not to tell them just before they go to bed, otherwise they may feel abandoned and alone as they lie awake worrying about what is going to happen.

If you can tell the children together it helps to have worked out what you are going to say, and to be in a position to tell them what your plans for the future are. If you have thought about what the contact arrangements will be, you can tell them. If they are old enough, you can discuss these with them. It is important, however, that they do not feel that they are being asked to take the responsibility for the decisions, although their wishes and feelings will be consulted.

The children's reaction

Even if your relationship with your partner has reached the point where you feel that you can no longer carry on living together, and the strains have become only too clear to you, you may well find that the prospect of a separation comes as a shock to the children. They may react with disbelief, denial and a frantic attempt to make it not happen.

Most children would rather keep their parents together at all costs, even when they know that they are unhappy together. Commonly, children will blame themselves for what has happened, deciding that their father or mother has left because of their behaviour. You may have the added complication of a different reaction from the children whom you share and your respective stepchildren. Try not to let the household divide into partisan camps. It is better if the children can be encouraged to seek a co-operative solution. If you have decided that you are going to separate and each take your own children with you, remember that the children may miss each other too. Sometimes stepbrothers and stepsisters form very strong friendships and alliances, and you need to consider how these can be preserved.

When you break the news to the children, it is important to stress that it is an adult decision, and that though you do not feel that you can go on living together, you still both love them very much and are going to go on being their parents. This is a message that you will have to repeat many times. Tempting as it is to lay blame, especially if you feel that your partner is the one at fault, try to keep blame out of it as far as the children are concerned.

Younger children

Younger children may well not understand very much of what is involved, though some may already have encountered other children whose parents are separated or divorced. You will need to explain the situation in words that they can understand, and it is tempting to fudge the issue and not tell the whole truth – to suggest that a separation will only be for a little while, when you yourselves know that it will be permanent. It is probably better to be honest at this stage rather than let the children cling to a false hope that will eventually disappoint them.

It is worth remembering that if 'courts' or 'law' are mentioned children tend to think only about criminal law and prison, so any reference of this kind can be much more alarming than you may expect.

Older children

Older children will be used to being consulted about their wishes in many family decisions. They may be very clear about which parent they want to live with or the sort of contact (access) they want to have. Try very hard, however, not to let them feel that they are being asked to choose between you and your partner. It is not fair to burden them with such a choice; they need to be reassured that adults will be responsible for the arrangements you make.

Older children will often have fairly complicated social lives of their own; adults need to remember this and respect the commitments that they already have. They may wish to live with one parent for a few years and then change to the other.

Young adults

It is tempting to think that once the children have reached the age of 18 and left home for college, a separation will not affect them so much. Many couples preserve a failing relationship until the youngest child has gone to college, or left home, for this reason. However, people in their late teens and early twenties can be very badly upset by their parents splitting up. It can be particularly hard for them if the home that they have known disappears while they are away, the bedrooms that they regard as theirs are no longer as they left them, the neighbourhood that they grew up in is lost.

Try to bear in mind that although in the eyes of the law your youngsters may be adults, they are still very dependent on you and it will be better if you can tell them together, and when they are at home, not while they are away at college or right at the end of the holiday, so that they go back to college to face the shock alone.

What you can do to help

The following is a list (not exhaustive) of various suggestions:

- Tell the schools as soon as you have told the children, or even in advance. It is bound to affect their school work or behaviour to some extent. If the school knows, they will be sympathetic and do what they can to help.
- Try to keep domestic routines as they were. Try to maintain your normal attitude to discipline and behaviour. It is tempting to be super-indulgent to try to make up for the hurt. But children rely on routine and frameworks to reinforce their sense of order in the world. You have already broken part of their world order; try to keep the rest of it in place.
- You need to talk to the children a lot, but try not to confide in them in the way that you would with an adult friend. They do not need the burden of the intimate detail of your relationship, tempting as it is to justify your side of the story.
- Go on referring to your partner as you did before. Don't use terms such as 'that man', or 'that *****, your mother'. Don't go unnaturally formal either: 'Mr Smith', 'Ms Jones'. Your children can do without this.
- Treats are a good idea, but spoiling isn't. Don't start buying expensive presents as compensation, or bribery. Children know when they are being bought and can be quite cold-blooded about exploiting the situation.
- Take advantage of any offer of adult help that you can get. If friends offer to take the children out to let you have a rest, accept gratefully. Life as a single parent is very hard work. It is not an admission of failure to accept help.
- Widen the family circle. It is easy to retreat into your small family world when a separation hits you, but this can be very claustrophobic and make you more miserable. Instead, try to invite the children's friends home, and get other adults to come round. If

you can keep your home an open, friendly place, the children will find it easier to adjust to the new situation.

- Children can be greatly helped by adult friends of their own. Grandparents, aunts and uncles, godparents and other family friends can be very helpful confidants (provided they can be persuaded not to take sides). Your children may find it easier to talk to them than to you. This is not because they don't love you; it is because they feel that they do not want to burden you with their troubles.

How the law works

Chapter 4 describes how parental responsibility works. The Children Act 1989 also covers situations where parents are separated and cannot agree about the arrangements for their children.

The expectation of the Children Act was that, for the most part, parents are capable of deciding matters for their children without the intervention of the courts. The old terms of 'custody', 'care and control' and 'access' have been abolished (although journalists still use them). If parents can agree arrangements for where the children will live ('residence') and how they will see the parent whom they do not live with ('contact'), the court will not make any order about this. Orders will only be made where parents cannot reach an agreement about the arrangements, and only then if the existence of the order is felt by the judge to be necessary to keep the parents from further dispute.

Residence

You will need to decide where the children are going to make their main home. This is often fairly obvious, with most children staying in the original family home. But other arrangements can be made. If you are going to move them out of their family home, do remember that they will need their own things with them. Children have close and intense relationships with their own possessions. (Look how refugee children will cling to their toys.) Make sure that they are allowed to take with them whatever they feel they need, even if you think that what they want to bring is junk. We all have the need for our own clutter.

Some families will feel that the children can have two 'main' homes and divide their time equally between their parents. If this is your feeling, you need to be absolutely sure that you are not treating the children as an asset that you want to divide equally between you. Think how you would feel if you had to move home every three or four days. Is it likely to be unsettling for them? It is not helpful if you make the decision on the basis of what you feel is 'fair' for you.

Contact

'Contact', as the term is used in the Children Act, can mean anything from long overnight visits to telephone calls and letters. There is no single pattern of contact that is laid down or approved in any official way. Each family must make its own arrangements. Whatever you can agree can later be altered to suit changes in the children's interests, or domestic arrangements, for instance.

Arrangements for contact

Contact can produce all sorts of troubles of its own, so the following is a list of helpful tips.

- Regular arrangements are best. You know where you stand as parents, and the children find that they have a framework they can rely on, providing everybody sticks to them.

- At the same time, don't be horribly rigid. If there is a special occasion to which your child should go and it clashes with a contact visit, try to be flexible and rearrange the visit.

- Get a large write-on calendar, and jointly plan the contact times ahead. The children can put stickers on the contact days and this helps them to keep track of their weeks.

- In the early days of a separation, it may not be possible to sort out a regular pattern of contact: both your lives may be in too much upheaval. You might be tempted to say that you will not have contact for a while because you fear that it will disrupt the children too much, where the reality is that you are the one more likely to be upset. Try to start by keeping contact; eventually a regular pattern can emerge. The children will need you very much at this time in their lives.

- It is very important to be careful about time-keeping. If you agree to collect or return children at particular times, you should stick to this. Similarly, if the children are being collected from you, you should have them ready at the correct time. Nothing annoys the other parent more than being careless about this. And the children, too, will be upset if you do not come when they expect you. With mobile phones so readily available there can hardly be an excuse these days for not warning the other if something has unexpectedly caused a delay.

- Don't complain about the other parent when you have the children with you. Also, don't use the children as a way of keeping tabs on what your partner is doing. Children know when they are being used as spies, and it is unfair to pull their loyalties in two directions.

- 'Contact', says the law, is the child's right to see the parent, and not the other way about. It is worth remembering this.
- Telephone calls can be very useful as a way of keeping in touch, but if you are the one phoning the child, try to agree with your partner about when would be a useful time.
- Try not to turn every contact visit into a wild outing somewhere. Low-key activities, such as drawing, painting and reading together, may be just as pleasurable for your child. What they want is your time and attention; don't substitute the spending of money for the giving of love.
- When children come back from a contact visit they are often cross, fractious and over-excited. It is easy to feel that this must be because the contact visit is doing them harm, and try to stop it. But children are like this at the end of any hectic day. Remember what it was like when you were all together. Don't put all the blame on your partner, or the visit. They may be a little more upset because the handover from one parent to another reminds them of what they have lost, but this does not mean that contact is something traumatic that should be avoided – even if they do behave terribly when they get home.
- If you are the non-resident parent it is easy to feel that you have lost, or are losing, your relationship with your children. Of course things are now different, but children are capable of sustaining close and intimate relationships with people that they do not see every day, and loving them very much. If you are living a long way away from your children there is the telephone (and email, and even video links for some families). Children love to receive letters, or picture postcards when they are too small to read.
- As children get older they may get very full social calendars of their own. There will be after-school activities like Scouts and Guides and weekend ones like football. Somehow, you need to balance all these, and accept, if you have contact visits at the weekend, that you will need to take them to their activities as well.

Do we need a court order?

If you can agree what the arrangements are to be, you do not need to make an application to the court. The only exception to this is if you want to share parental responsibility with someone who is not the child's natural father (see Chapter 4); in this case you would need an order, but in most cases you are probably not going to face contested proceedings.

What if we can't agree?

Perhaps surprisingly, most parents do agree the arrangements for their children, and find a way of dealing with contact and residence. This is not to say that it will all be straightforward; there are bound to be extremely tricky times when you quarrel and everybody gets very upset.

Try to focus on the long term. Remember that you both have the children's interests at heart. If you can, make use of mediation to resolve disputes. If all else fails, you may have to use the court, but the court too will try to resolve issues by mediation.

Disputes about children

Under the Children Act 1989, the courts have wide powers to make orders for children. However, the court always has to consider whether, on balance, it would be better for the children to have no order made, rather than an order imposed. The whole focus of the Act is on helping parents to take responsibility for their children. If you do need an order, you will apply under section 8 of the Act, which lists the orders that the court can make; they are often referred to as 'section 8 orders'.

- **Residence order**: This states where the children make their main home, and with whom. Normally one parent will have this order, as it generally seems a bad idea to parcel a child out between two homes. Two people in one household can have a shared residence order, however. Parental responsibility automatically comes with a residence order. The reverse is not the case; parental responsibility does not automatically have residence with it.
- **Contact order**: This states what contact the person with whom the child lives should allow to the person who applies for contact. Contact can be in any form, so can include overnight stays, visits, telephone calls, letters and parcels. It may be very precisely defined by the court, with dates and times laid down, and who is to collect and deliver the child. For the most part, however, courts prefer to be less specific, in the hope that parents will work sensibly within the spirit of the order.
- **Specific issue order**: A court can be asked to decide a specific question where parents with parental responsibility cannot agree about an arrangement for a child, such as the school that he or she should go to.
- **Prohibited steps order**: This sort of order stops or restrains the way in which one parent is exercising parental responsibility. For instance it can be used to prevent a child being taken out of the country.

Applying for an order

How to apply

Almost anyone who is interested in the welfare of the child can apply to the court for a section 8 order for residence or contact. This includes: a parent; a guardian; a person with whom the child has lived for three of the last five years and within the last three months; any person who has the consent of the people or person who has parental responsibility. Anyone who does not fit into these categories must first get the permission of the court to make an application. This will normally be granted if it appears that the application may serve the child's welfare.

You make the application by filling in an application form C1. There are three helpful leaflets: 'Children and the Family Courts', 'Filling in the forms', and 'Serving the forms', and you can get these from the court or download them from the Court Service website.* You will need to have at least three copies of form C1, one for the court, one for your records and one for service on any person who already has parental responsibility for the child. The form asks for all the details of the child or children and asks you to say what sort of order you want made. There is a very small section for you to say why you want the order made. This is deliberate; at this stage the court does not want long and detailed evidence filed. If the case cannot be resolved at an early stage you will have the opportunity to set out your reasons in greater detail.

The proceedings have been designed to be accessible to people who are not used to the law. You should fill the form in carefully to make sure that all the facts are correct, but if you ask for the wrong order the court has power to correct an application, or even make an order that it has not been asked for.

Directions (or conciliation) appointment

The first stage is that the court will fix a 'directions appointment' or a 'conciliation appointment'. You and your partner (and any other person who has been served with the application), and your solicitors (if you have them), will be asked to attend an appointment before the district judge. This is in the judge's room, in private, as all hearings under the Children Act are. There will also be a court welfare officer, who is someone trained and experienced in dealing with children's legal issues.

In most courts you will be asked to go with your partner to talk to the court welfare officer privately. Legal advisers are generally left out of this meeting. The court welfare officer will try to explore with you what the issues and difficulties are. If possible, he or she will be trying to see whether an agreement could be reached. This is really a compressed form of mediation, and there will be quite a lot of pressure on you both to try to reach an agreement. For this reason alone, it would be sensible to try to use mediation first, before you get to the stage of filing an application.

If you can reach an agreement, then the district judge will be told what you have agreed. You may feel at this stage that you only want to agree to a short-term arrangement, to try it out. Most judges will understand this and think it is sensible. You could, for instance, agree to a pattern of contact visits for the next three months. The judge can then fix another appointment at the court that you can make use of if you want to. During the trial period you may well find that you can start to look ahead and agree plans for the future. The judge, in discussion with you and your legal advisers, has to decide whether it would be better to make no order (simply recording what has been agreed in a note on the file) or whether you need an order. The bias is always towards making no order, but if you have had a very difficult time in the past, and one or other of you has not been reliable at keeping to agreements, the judge may feel that an order would help you both to know where you stand.

The large majority of applications for section 8 orders stop at this stage, with an agreement being reached, or a temporary arrangement being put in place to see how things work.

Short-term arrangements

In the minority of cases, where the conciliation process has not been successful, the judge will then decide whether any short-term orders or arrangements should be made, pending a final decision of the court. He or she will make an order about who is to file evidence and by when. The judge will also order that a court welfare officer (a different officer from the one you have seen) should prepare a report about the children. Time limits will be set for the filing of documents and the next hearings. These must be strictly complied with, because the Children Act recognises that delay can be prejudicial to the welfare of the children. The welfare report can take several weeks to prepare however, because of the pressures that the service (the Children and Family Court Advisory and Support Service, CAFCASS) is under.

The welfare officer will interview all the adult parties to the case. He or she will also talk to the children; the older they are the greater the weight that the court will attach to their feelings and opinions. The welfare officer can also interview other people such as teachers, the family doctor, grandparents. The report that he or she prepares should set out the factual circumstances and give his or her opinion of how the interests of the child would be best served. If the welfare officer makes a recommendation the court will give this very serious consideration, but is not bound to follow it. Your solicitor will be sent a copy of the report once it is filed at court (or it will be sent to you if you are not legally represented). It will have a strong warning on it that it must not be shown to any third party without the permission of the court. This must be taken seriously and you should not show it to anyone else.

You will have the opportunity to file your own statement of evidence with the court. You should try to be careful to keep this to the facts as you see them. Avoid emotional arguments, angry adjectives, and abusing your former partner. The focus of what you say should be the children, and what is best for them. The court will not 'award' contact or residence as compensation for the pain that you have suffered, or as a reward for your good behaviour.

The child's welfare is paramount

These are factors that the court has to take into account in applying the principle that 'the child's welfare shall be the court's paramount consideration' (sometimes called the 'checklist'):

- the ascertainable wishes and feelings of the child (in the light of the child's age and understanding) and the child's physical, emotional and educational needs
- the likely effect on the child of any change in circumstances
- the child's age, sex, and background, and any characteristics that the court considers relevant
- any harm the child has suffered or is at risk of suffering
- the ability of each of the child's parents, and of any other person in relation to whom the court considers the question to be relevant, to meet the child's needs
- the range of powers available to the court.

Directions hearing

Once reports and statements of evidence have been filed, there is generally a second procedural hearing – often referred to as a 'directions hearing' – to make sure whether the case is going to proceed or not. If it is, the judge will direct whether any further evidence is needed and fix a time and date for the final hearing. However, a good many cases will be settled at this stage, once everyone concerned has had a chance to see the evidence and the welfare report. If the welfare report makes a strong recommendation for a particular sort of order, it may seem better not to fight a case if you think that the judge might not do what you would prefer. If you have a solicitor, he or she will be able to say what your chances of success are at this point, or whether it is still unpredictable. If you are publicly funded and your chances of success are poor, then your solicitor will be under a duty to report this to the Community Legal Service,* which can refuse to fund your case further if it seems that it would be more sensible to settle it at this stage.

Once an order or agreement has been made

As children get older, so arrangements and even court orders need to be modified to accommodate their new needs and, often, their out-of-school activities. If you simply have agreed residence and contact, you can revise and adapt your arrangements as the years pass. If you get to the point where you can no longer agree you can, as a last resort, apply to the court to settle the matter as outlined above.

If you started off with a court order, and circumstances change so that it no longer seems appropriate, you do not have to return to the court to change it; if by this stage you can reach an agreement, you can simply introduce the modifications that you both want. If you cannot agree how it should be changed, you can go back to the court. The same procedure will apply, so it would be sensible to see if mediation would help you first.

Capital orders for children

If you need a lump sum from your partner for your child or children, or need to try to preserve the family home for them, you need to take legal advice about the best way of proceeding. Tactically it may be a good idea to combine an application for the children – if they are going to live with you – with any claim that you may have for a share in the family home. The children's rights are dealt with under the Children Act 1989, which does not cover applications by parents on their own account, so you would be asking the court to make orders under two different sets of powers. With good legal advice you can proceed in the most advantageous way for your particular set of circumstances.

Although the court's powers to make maintenance orders for children have been largely taken over by the Child Support Agency (see Chapter

13), the court still has powers to make orders for lump-sum payments and transfers of property. A transfer of property can include the transfer of a tenancy in a rented property, as well as the ownership of a house or flat. The Child Support Agency does not deal with capital payments.

You can get a capital order only against a parent (by blood or adoption); a step-parent in an unmarried family cannot be ordered to pay for a child who is not his or hers. However, courts generally do not take the view that it is a good thing for a child to receive a large capital sum, or to have property transferred. (A child cannot hold real property in any event, so an adult would have to be appointed as trustee until the child reached 18.) In some circumstances, however, a capital sum may be appropriate. A typical example might be where a child needed a particular piece of expensive equipment, such as a disabled child needing a computer; or a child needing particular adaptations to accommodation if he or she were disabled. If a couple have split up before the birth of a child or shortly after, a lump sum may be appropriate to pay for the mass of baby equipment that a new child seems to need – car seat, cot, buggy, and so on. Sometimes it may be a good idea to provide a lump sum for future school fees. You cannot, however, have a series of lump-sum payments instead of maintenance.

A transfer-of-property order in favour of a child is even more unusual, but the power is there; if an application for an order in favour of a child or children is combined with an application by the parent with whom they are going to live over the former family home, this can be quite effective. Lawyers might regard this as a 'belt and braces' approach. The problem from the court's point of view is that if property is transferred to the children, once they are 18 they are entitled to it absolutely and this means they can sell it; since the court does not have power to provide for adult children (unless they are disabled), an order that achieved this result would be wrong. A court will therefore, under the Children Act, generally order property to be held by both or one parent so that it is the children's home while they are under 18 or still in full-time education, and the court will say what should happen to it after that time.

It also seems to be generally agreed that it is a bad idea for children to come into too much money at 18, and that they should be protected from the risks that such sudden affluence might create. Some parents, however, would rather transfer property to their children than to their estranged partners, despite the later risks. If you and your partner are trying to reach an agreement without invoking the power of the court, this may seem to be an attractive option, but do bear in mind the effect on the children later on.

A fair deal for the whole family

Annie says: 'When Mike and I split up the kids were eight and ten. The house was in our joint names and we reckoned that we had made equal contributions. We agreed that I would stay in the house with the children and Mike wanted to give his half of the house to the children – he certainly wasn't going to agree that I would have it. I didn't think that this would be a good idea. I didn't want to get into the situation where they wanted to force a sale and I was opposing them over this. You know what kids are like when they are 18 and want to buy things like cars and motorbikes, or even have to fund themselves through college.

In the end we did what I thought was a better deal. We put the house in my sole name, so that Mike could get another house with a mortgage. But Mike had a charge over it for a third of its value. We both promised that we would make wills leaving our share in the house to the children. Mike promised to pay his share of the mortgage until the children got to 18 or finished at university. I was given the option of buying him out at that stage, or selling the house and paying him his third. We felt that that way the children would not lose out if either of us started to live with someone else.'

An application for a capital order or a transfer-of-property order for children is made under the Children Act 1989. The parent with whom the child is living normally makes the application. The usual Children Act application form, C1, has to be filed, together with a supplementary form C10 that sets out the orders that you are asking the court to make, and C10A which is your statement of means. (All these forms are available from your local county court, or from the court service website: www.courtservice.gov.uk) The court fixes the timetable for the hearing, much as it does if you are applying for an order about residence or contact. Your partner will also have to file a C10 form about his or her means. Other evidence will be filed as agreed or ordered by the court.

Chapter 13

Child support

The child support legislation, which all springs from the Child Support Act 1991 and has since been amended, applies only to a parent-child relationship. Under the law you cannot be made to pay for a stepchild: only for your own child, by blood or adoption. The Act operates only when you are separated and no longer living in the same household as the child. The new rules of child support are due to come into effect in April 2002, and will be introduced gradually; although some readers will be paying under the old rules, the old system is not described in any detail here. If you have already been affected by the Child Support Agency* (CSA), *The Which? Guide to Divorce* sets out the old law.

This chapter first describes the ideas behind the legislation and the technical terms that the child support system uses. It then deals with the law as it is intended to be from April 2002.

Getting advice about the Child Support Agency

Solicitors, the Citizens Advice Bureaux and some law centres should be able to offer advice and help about getting or paying child support through the CSA. Many of them will have computer programs that will enable them to check a maintenance assessment or calculation, or work out for you what the likely impact of an application would be. Solicitors will be able to offer a limited amount of advice under the Legal Help scheme, but they cannot generally help you complete the application form, or the enquiry form. They would be able to advise over particular legal points such as paternity, or jurisdiction.

Public funding (the new term for legal aid) is not available to help you challenge a CSA assessment through most of the initial appeal stages: reviewing an assessment, appealing to the Child Support Appeals tribunal or to the Child Support Commissioner. Only if you get past these stages, and have to make an application to the court on a point of law, will public funding be available.

A solicitor can assist you with these steps under the Legal Help scheme and could also assist you – though not represent you – as what is known as a 'McKenzie friend', at a tribunal hearing. Public funding is available for taking a case about paternity to the courts.

The CSA helpline also offers advice, but you may get an answer only on general points, not for your particular circumstances.

The Child Support Act 1991

The Child Support Act 1991 set up the Child Support Agency,★ which started operating on 5 April 1993. It was set up to take over responsibility for child maintenance applications, and the intention was that it would take them out of the hands of the courts. One of the principal aims of the Act was to recoup for the Treasury the money that was being paid out in the benefit system to single parents. By pursuing 'non-resident parents', as the Act called them, and obtaining maintenance from them, it was hoped that single parents would be 'floated off' income-support levels.

In order to achieve this, a complicated formula was devised by which the maintenance payable could be calculated. Because of the aim of relieving the income support system, the figures that were used in the maintenance calculation were drawn from the social security allowances. This means that they are revised each year in line with the figures from the Department of Work and Pensions (DWP).★

The old formula proved to be a problem. It was impossible to work out at a glance what maintenance should be paid; you needed to have detailed information about both parties' finances to be able to do this. The possibilities for error were numerous, and the CSA has often itself got the calculations wrong. As a result, new rules, which are designed to be a great deal simpler, are being introduced and will apply from April 2002.

Originally it was intended that the CSA would deal with all cases of maintenance for children, but the numbers made this unworkable. People in receipt of benefit are obliged to use the CSA to pursue their partners for child maintenance. People who are not in receipt of benefit were originally, under the 1991 Act, given a transitional period in which they could choose whether to use the CSA or the courts. However, the backlog of benefit cases so overwhelmed the CSA that the transitional period was extended indefinitely. Although the power of the courts to hear a contested application for child maintenance has been removed, you can obtain a court order by agreeing the amounts and having this ratified as an order by the court. This is the route that most people who are not obliged to use the CSA have taken.

> **No gender distinction**
>
> This chapter refers to the non-resident parent as 'he' and 'him' and the parent with care as 'she' and 'her' throughout, because in the vast majority of cases this is how things are. However, the Act makes no distinction over gender, so if you are a male parent with care the formula and rules will be applied in exactly the same way.

The Child Support Agency (CSA)

The CSA calculates the maintenance according to the formula laid down in the Act and in subsequent legislation. It will trace the 'non-resident parent' and pursue him for maintenance. It has investigative powers to find out about a parent's income and capital. If the non-resident parent does not pay, it has powers to compel payment, the most effective of which is by direct deduction from wages. The new legislation also gives the court power to disqualify him from driving.

Terminology and jurisdiction

These are the terms used, and what they mean:

- *The non-resident parent*   A parent (either by blood or adoption) who no longer lives in the same household as the child for whom the maintenance is applied. (Step-parents are not responsible for the maintenance of their stepchildren under the CSA.)
- *The parent/person with care*   The person whom the child lives with and who has the usual day-to-day care of the child. If both parents care for the child from time to time, the parent who gets the child benefit becomes the parent with care.
- *The qualifying child*   The child must be under 16, or under 19 but still in full-time, secondary education.
- *Habitual residence*   The child and both the parents must all be habitually resident in the UK. 'Habitual residence' means usual residence with a settled intention to remain. If the non-resident parent is abroad, the CSA cannot deal with maintenance and the court will have to deal with it instead. However, if the non-resident parent is employed by a British company, the CSA can take action against him.

Who uses the CSA?

If you had a written agreement for maintenance for the children before 5 April 1993 (this is becoming a smaller group of parents each year), you cannot make an application to the CSA. This rule is over-ridden if the parent with care goes onto benefit.

Parents with care who are in receipt of income support and jobseeker's allowance are obliged to ask the CSA to make an assessment of maintenance against the non-resident parent. (This used to apply also to recipients of family credit – now known as working families tax credit – and recipients of disability working allowance, but the rules have now changed.) If the parent with care is not prepared to co-operate with the CSA then her benefit can be reduced – by 40 per cent of the income support adult personal allowance (£21.58 per week in 2002–3) for up to three years.

Parents with care who are not on benefit are not compelled to use the system. It is recognised that the CSA will not be able to cope with all separated parents, and the government states that it wants to encourage people to reach agreements. You can make a private agreement if the parent with care is not on benefit (as described) and you can ask a court to make a maintenance order in the terms that you have agreed. Under the old rules the existence of a court order would stop you applying to the CSA (unless the parent with care went onto benefit), but this rule has now been changed.

The CSA will offer a collection service to people who have reached their own agreements, but only for collecting maintenance at CSA rates. The effect of this would be that CSA assessments would replace the court order or agreement if private payment arrangements broke down. The plan is that these proposals will not apply to existing court orders or agreements: they will be available only after the reforms come into effect, that is, to agreements or orders made after April 2002. In addition, CSA collection and assessment services will be available only after a court order has been in place for at least a year.

Parents who wish to transfer from a private agreement or court order to a child support assessment will have to give at least two months' notice. This will allow parents and their lawyers time to rene-gotiate new voluntary agreements if appropriate. The government White Paper in which the new scheme was set out stated: 'We believe that these proposals will encourage parents, lawyers and the Courts to come to child maintenance arrangements in the shadow of the CSA. All parties will know that either parent can turn to the CSA in future, and that it would therefore be sensible to determine child maintenance broadly in line with CSA assessment rates. The Courts would still be free, as now, to determine spousal maintenance, property and pension settlements for the couple concerned.'

Since the 1991 Act came into force the courts have no power to deal with a *new* contested application for child maintenance. If parents can reach an agreement about maintenance for the children, the terms of this can be made into a court order under Schedule 1 of the Children Act 1989 'by consent'. However, the court does still have power to *vary* a court order. This means that if an order is made by consent, either party can later apply to the court for it to be varied: either increased or decreased. It has become a reasonably common practice for couples to agree a basic child maintenance order and have it made in the court by consent so that, if they cannot resolve their differences about maintenance, they can invoke the power of the court to order a variation.

It makes sense, when agreeing an order by consent, to do a calculation of maintenance, using the CSA formula, to make sure that the figure that you agree is broadly in line with what you might get from the CSA. However, this figure might be altered by other parts of any settlement that you are discussing.

The effect of the CSA has been to create a two-tier system, with one law for those in receipt of benefit, and a more flexible system for those who are not. This is not a happy result, from the politicians' point of view, but it seems to be accepted that the task of dealing with all maintenance cases is not one that the CSA can reasonably be expected to take on in the foreseeable future.

How to apply for maintenance

Either parent can apply for a maintenance assessment, though normally it will be the parent with care. An application can be made as soon as the parents separate. You can get an application form from your local DWP office, by writing to or telephoning your CSA branch office, or by downloading it from the DWP website★. The old form is very long and detailed, though it should become considerably shorter and simpler once the new scheme is in force.

Once the application has been made, the non-resident parent will get an equally long form to complete and send back. If he delays the CSA can levy an interim assessment, often at punitive rates. This is intended to encourage a quick response.

Fees

There is no fee payable at present, though there is power in the legislation for a fee to be charged. The fees had to be waived in 1997, because the service was becoming so inadequate, and they have not been reinstated. They were originally £34 for assessment and £44 for collection.

How maintenance is calculated

Net income

Net income means your weekly income (including overtime) after deduction of income tax and National Insurance contributions. You can also deduct any contribution to a pension scheme. However, if a parent with care thinks that the non-resident parent has unreasonably diverted income into a pension scheme to avoid paying maintenance, she will be able to apply to have the child support rates varied to reflect this. The basic rates will take no account of any income that the non-resident parent has from savings and investments. However, if a non-resident parent gets most of his income from this source, the parent with care will be able to apply for a variation of the liability, as with other cases where the non-resident parent's lifestyle is inconsistent with his assessed income.

In calculating income the CSA will also ignore child benefit and non-contributory benefits for disabled people (such as disability living allowance and attendance allowance), housing benefit and council tax benefit. The agency will also ignore income from boarders (unless it is a significant source of income) and student loans and grants. However, tax credits received in the pay packet, such as working families tax credit, will be treated as part of income (unless they are paid to the non-resident parent's new partner in his or her wage packet).

Basic rate

Maintenance will be calculated by taking a proportion of the non-resident parent's net weekly income. This is called the 'basic rate':

- 15 per cent for one qualifying child
- 20 per cent for two qualifying children
- 25 per cent for three or more qualifying children.

If the non-resident parent has other children (called 'relevant children') for whom he or his new partner (in a male/female partnership) receives child benefit (such as new children or stepchildren from a second marriage or cohabitation), the rate of maintenance is calculated by applying the percentages above to the net income after first deducting a similar percentage for the relevant child or children. So if a father had one child by his first partner and one by his second, you would take away 15 per cent from his net income (as a notional amount for the second child) and then the maintenance for the first child would be 15 per cent of what is left.

Reduced rate

If the non-resident parent's net weekly income is more than £100 but less than £200, he will pay a 'reduced rate'.

Reduced rate calculation

If net income is more than £100 per week and less than £200 apply the following formula to find the weekly maintenance:

F (Flat rate: £5) + (A (Net income) × T (see table below))

---

	1 qualifying child				2 qualifying children				3 qualifying children			
Number of relevant children of the non-resident parent	0	1	2	3+	0	1	2	3+	0	1	2	3+
T (%)	25	20.5	19	17.5	35	29	27	25	45	37.5	35	32.5

Flat rate

Maintenance will be payable at a 'flat rate' of £5 per week if the non-resident parent's net weekly income is £100 or less, or he is in receipt of:

- income support
- jobseeker's allowance
- retirement pension
- incapacity benefit
- contribution-based jobseeker's allowance
- widow's benefits
- severe disablement allowance
- invalid care allowance
- industrial injuries disablement benefit
- war pension.

Nil rate

For some non-resident parents there will be a 'nil rate' payable: this will be for people who have income of less than £5 per week, prisoners, children aged 16–17 and those in receipt of student grants or loans or youth training allowances.

Apportionment: children with different parents with care

Where a non-resident parent has children who have different parents with care, the amount of child support payable is apportioned between the different parents with care. The amount payable is divided by the number of children and shared depending on how many children each parent with care has.

Shared care: basic and reduced rate

If you share the care of the child or children, so that from time to time they stay overnight with the non-resident parent, this will decrease the amount of maintenance payable. You have to look at the number of nights that the children have spent with the non-resident parent over the last 12 months, or, if the break-up is new, the projected number of nights in the next year. The reductions are:

Number of nights	Subtract
52 to 103	one-seventh
104 to 155	two-sevenths
156 to 174	three-sevenths
175 or more	one-half

Take each child and add the number of sevenths together, then divide that by the number of children. If the fraction that you end up with is one-half, then you also reduce the maintenance by £7 per week for that child.

Example

If you have one child whose reduction is one-seventh and another whose reduction is two-sevenths, add these and divide by two. This gives you a reduction of $\frac{3}{14}$.

The lower limit to which the maintenance can be decreased is £5 per week. (If there are children with different parents with care, the £5 minimum is divided as described above.)

Shared care: flat rate

If the child or children spend at least 52 nights a year with the non-resident parent, and this parent would otherwise be paying at the flat rate (see 'Flat rate' above), the maintenance reduces to nil.

Transitional provisions

People who have already got CSA assessments running will be switched to the new system. The White Paper recognised that this might cause a change in the amount payable that would lead to hardship if the change was implemented at once, so there are transitional provisions.

Where net income is £100 a week or less – or if the non-resident parent is on benefit – the new assessment will be phased in by steps, starting with £2.50 a week. In these cases, where there is no liability under the existing child support scheme, a non-resident parent will have to pay only £2.50 a week, rather than the new liability of £5, for the first year. Where the non-resident parent's net income is between £100 and £400 a week, the assessment will be phased in by steps starting with £5 a week for the first year; and for non-resident parents earning £400 per week or more, the new assessment will be phased in by steps starting with £10.

Variations and departures from assessments

In some cases, where the formula does not appear to produce an appropriate amount of maintenance, you can apply to the CSA for a variation. Under the previous law this was called a 'departure direction'.

If the non-resident parent has special expenses that are related to the children, such as the costs of contact arrangements (for example fares, or petrol), the CSA can take this into account and reduce the assessment. Boarding school fees can also be taken into account. So can mortgage payments if the non-resident parent is making these for the former family home and no longer has an interest in that property.

The assessment can also be varied if the calculation does not reflect the non-resident parent's true ability to pay. This may be where he has considerable capital assets (which do not come into the formula). The level in the regulations is £65,000 of capital. The assessment may also be varied where the non-resident parent has sporadic or discretionary income that does not normally get counted into the formula.

Chapter 14

Your interests in the home

The basic principle is that when cohabitants split up there are no rules in the law to say that either has to make a payment to the other of any sort, either of capital or income. This means that neither has an obligation to pay maintenance to the other (see Chapter 16). It also means that when it comes to sorting out property, you can only sort out things that you have owned jointly (or, in a limited set of circumstances, that are treated as joint property). So property that has always been in your sole name, and that you have never made any pretence of sharing and that your partner has made no contribution to, remain your sole property and your partner cannot claim them from you.

If it is death that ends the partnership, rather than separation, the bereaved partner does have some rights, however, to claim a share in the deceased's estate. That situation is outlined in Chapter 5. This chapter deals with the division of the home; the next chapter deals with contents and other jointly owned items.

If you made a living together agreement with a declaration of trust in your home, or just a declaration of trust in your home, and you are happy to abide by your original agreement about the division of the home, then you will have saved yourselves a great deal of time and legal costs and you can happily ignore the rest of this chapter. If you have not done this, it is important to read the chapter even if you are not currently considering splitting up, to make yourself aware of the legal minefield that may lie before you if you do not sort out the ownership of your home.

The rights of cohabitants to the home in which they have lived together are not clear-cut. There is no convenient Act that sets out the law or regulates your rights and duties to each other. Instead, there are a number of Acts which have some bearing on the legal problem, there are numerous cases (each of which hinges on its own facts), and there is what lawyers call 'common law and equity' – the principles of law that have evolved over the last centuries. Through all this you and your lawyers will have to pick your way. This chapter may therefore seem confusing: it can give you only an outline of the principles that the law will apply. You will probably need good legal advice tailored to your particular situation.

A home that you own

Different considerations apply to your home depending on whether you own or rent it. This section deals with property that you own, whether jointly or in one person's name. This could be a freehold or what is called a 'long leasehold'.

Separation

This part of the chapter explains the situation if you separate. Different rules apply on death; the situation on death is outlined in Chapter 5 and in the section headed 'Death' below.

There are also different legal positions depending on whether you hold the home in your joint names or it is in one person's name.

The home is in your joint names

There are two ways of holding your home jointly. The two legal terms are 'joint tenancy' and 'tenancy in common'. In a joint tenancy the shares that you each hold are not treated as separate. When one of you dies the other automatically inherits the other's share. You cannot give your share to anyone else, in a will or during your lifetime. You would normally be treated as owning equal shares in the home, so you would each be entitled to 50 per cent if the home were sold. If you originally agreed to a joint tenancy, then the presumption is that you wanted to share the home equally. A court may be able to rearrange the shares, however, if you did not intend to share the property equally.

In a tenancy in common your shares are your individual property, so that you can leave your share of the home to someone in a will, for instance. You do not necessarily have to hold the home in equal shares. When you bought the home the shares in which you held it should have been set out in a declaration of trust. If there is no declaration, then the general presumption is that you do hold it in equal shares, but a court can change this, as described below.

What does a 'common intention' mean?

Miss Springette and Mr Defoe lived together for three years. The council house into which they had moved as joint tenants was offered to them under the 'right to buy' scheme. They raised a mortgage together, but Miss Springette provided almost all of the deposit from her savings, and the council discount that they were offered was attributable to Miss Springette's status as a long-standing council tenant, not Mr Defoe's. In all, Miss Springette contributed about 75 per cent of the purchase price. However, when they bought the house it was put into their joint names as joint tenants, effectively giving it to them in equal shares. There was no declaration about the contribution that each had made.

When the relationship broke up about three years after the purchase, Mr Defoe went to court to try to get his share of the house. The judge who heard the case to start with took the view that as the house had been put into joint names they were entitled to equal shares, despite the unequal contributions, because this must have been their 'common intention'.

Luckily for Miss Springette, the Court of Appeal took a different view and said that you could not have a 'common intention' if you had not communicated this to each other. One judge said, 'Our trust law does not allow property rights to be affected by telepathy.' As there was no evidence that the couple had discussed that they would share the property equally, they were entitled to the house in the shares in which they had contributed.

The crucial point to note in this case is that there was evidence that the couple had never discussed how they were going to hold the property. In most relationships it will be hard to establish a negative like this; if you have talked about buying a home together, you are likely to have discussed how you will own it. It is always better to be explicit, and if possible record your intentions in writing. Miss Springette may have won the larger share, but it took six years to get to the Court of Appeal judgement, and the costs must have been considerable.

Did you have a declaration of trust or a different sort of agreement about how you held the home?

When you bought the home jointly, or transferred it from one of you into your joint names, you should have been advised about the legal implications and a declaration of trust should have been drawn up. In

English law, property that is held in joint names is said to be held 'on trust'. If you are joint owners you are treated as holding the property on trust for yourselves. You are the 'beneficiaries' of the trust.

If your solicitor did not draw up a declaration of trust, you may have the basis for a claim against the firm. See 'Do you have a remedy against the solicitors who helped you buy the home?', below.

If you had a declaration of trust, the straightforward position is that you stick with that division of the home. But in some circumstances the court may be prepared to rearrange your shares.

You do not have to have a formal declaration of trust to establish the shares in which you hold the home. You may have had some other sort of written agreement: a letter from one of you to the other might be enough. Or you can have had an oral agreement. This is of course more difficult to prove and would depend on the evidence that both of you gave. If you are both certain about the terms of your agreement, you would expect to be bound by it. But again, you or your partner might apply to the court to rearrange the shares if there were compelling reasons for it to do so.

The difficulty with an oral agreement, or even a loosely written one, is that very often there will be a difference between your two recollections of what was originally agreed. This may be because time has made your memories vague, or because we would always prefer a version of events that is broadly in our own favour. If you cannot agree, you may have to put it to a court, where the judge will have to decide whose evidence he or she finds the more convincing.

When a court can alter an agreement

There are two sets of circumstances where, despite an original agreement, you may end up having a legal dispute. The first is where the dispute is essentially about what the terms of the original agreement were. In these cases the court will have to conduct an investigation into the facts. In the absence of any other argument on either side, the court would declare your shares in the home to be as it finds they were originally arranged.

The second is where one or both of you argues that there is a very good reason for the court to judge that you can depart from the original agreement. This is likely to be for one of two main reasons. The first is where you have subsequently renegotiated the agreement. You may have formally recorded this renegotiation or you may have simply relied on what you thought was a mutual understanding that the situation had changed. Here again, the court would be concerned to establish what really happened between you, and divide the home accordingly. The second is where events or actions after the original agreement have been so inconsistent with the original agreement that the logical conclusion is that there must have been a variation or cancellation of the agreement. An example of this would be where you agreed to hold the house in equal shares on the understanding that you would both contribute equally to the purchase price and the mortgage; subsequently one of you has paid little or nothing. Here, the court would not only be looking at what had actually happened but also at what would be fair or appropriate, given the original intention of the agreement. The court can look at all the circumstances during your relationship, but one of the key factors will be the contribution that you have each made in money, or in kind, to the purchase or improvement of the home. Payments of money can be 'treated as illuminating the common intention as to the extent of the beneficial interest'.

What if you don't want the home sold?

So far, what we have been looking at is simply establishing who owns what share in the home. You may already agree about this, or you may need to negotiate it through lawyers, or even go to the extent of getting a court ruling on it. The next stage is to decide what is to happen to the home. If you both agree that it is to be sold, then things become relatively simple; once it is sold you divide the net proceeds according to your agreement or the decision of the court, and go your separate ways.

However, if one of you wants to sell and the other wants to stay in the home, what happens then? One way out of this is for the person who wants to stay to purchase the other's share at whatever price you can agree on. But you cannot always afford to do this.

Joint owners can sell property only by mutual agreement or by getting a court order that the property should be sold. Normally it will be the person who wants the property sold who applies to the court. These applications are made under the Trusts of Land and Appointment of Trustees Act 1996 (TOLATA). In every application for an order for sale, the court has to consider:

- the intentions of the person or persons who created the trust
- the purposes for which the property subject to the trust is held
- the welfare of any minor who occupies or might reasonably be expected to occupy any land subject to the trust as his home
- the interests of any secured creditor (such as the mortgage company) of any beneficiary.

This gives the court a good deal of flexibility in deciding whether or not to make an order for sale. If, for instance, you bought the house intending it to be a home for you and your children, you can argue that the house should not be sold until the children have grown up and no longer need it as a roof over their heads.

The home is in one person's name

Where the home is in the name of only one of you, the straightforward common-law position says that the non-owner has no interest in the home.

However, English law also has a set of what are called 'equitable principles'. These can override the common law to make sure that a fairer result is achieved. You have still to make sure that your case comes within the established criteria laid down as precedents by a whole line of previous cases.

The court looks at what has happened in your relationship to decide whether it can find that a 'trust' has been created. A trust in this context would mean that the ownership of the property should be shared in some way. The court can decide that there has been an 'express trust', which is nothing to do with its speed, but that it has been expressed or declared in some way: you could have done this in a living together agreement.

If there has not been an express trust, there may be an 'implied trust'. The court can take the view that there must, or ought to have been, a trust of the home because of the way that you have both behaved – for instance, if you both contributed to the payment when the house was bought, or to the mortgage repayments.

You may also be able either to claim a share of the sale proceeds, or to prevent the home being sold over your head, if you can rely on something called 'proprietary estoppel'. To be able to rely on this, you must show that the owner has behaved in such a way that you were led to believe that you would have a right in the home, whether to a share or to a right to occupy it; and that, based on this belief, you have acted to your detriment. You might have done this by making financial contributions to the home or by doing improvements to it. You need not always have made yourself financially worse off; you might, for instance, have given up your home and come to live with your partner, relying on his or her promises that you would have a home with him or her for life.

Was there an understanding or agreement?

You will need to establish what your original understanding or agreement was. This may not be disputed, but as you are both going to want a version of events which serves your own purposes best, there is

---

Proprietary estoppel: Kamilla's story

Kamilla Lesnoff was Polish. She had a secure tenancy of her flat in Wroclaw. She had gone back to university after her marriage ended, obtained a master's degree and seemed set on a promising academic career. Then she fell in love with Anatole Ungarian, who was Lebanese, and they set up home in London. Mrs Lesnoff gave up her flat in Poland and her career. Mr Ungarian bought a house for them in Muswell Hill; he bought it in his sole name. Mrs Lesnoff did a considerable amount of work on the house, which was in a poor state of repair. After the couple split up, Mrs Lesnoff remained in the house. Mr Ungarian tried to get an order for possession of it. The court held that it was the intention of the couple that Mrs Lesnoff should have the right to live in that house for her life; she had acted to her detriment in giving up her home and career in Poland, and she was entitled to be treated as if she was the 'tenant for life' (which means that she has the right to live there for the whole of her life).

---

likely to be an argument over the original facts. Unless you can agree, broadly speaking, on what was originally said, or implied, the court will have to make a finding about which version the judge thinks is the more probable.

Has the non-owner acted to his or her detriment?

The owner has to show what the non-owner has done in reliance on the promises. The latter might have paid towards the purchase of the home either directly, by contributing towards the purchase price, or by contributing to the mortgage payments. Or he or she might have made indirect payments, paying for something else that freed the owner's money so that it could be used for the purchase or mortgage payments. The non-owner might have helped with the cost of decorating or maintaining the home, or helped in kind, with repairs or renovations.

The non-owner might have made no actual contribution in this way, but still lost out as a result of his or her reliance on the owner. For example, he or she might have given up a home and job in order to live together, like Kamilla Lesnoff (see box).

What the court can do
The court can decide whether you ought to have a share in the home (and how big that share ought to be), or whether you have the right to live in the home for a fixed period, or for life.

> **An unreliable promise**
>
> In the case of *Wayling v Jones*, Mr Wayling succeeded in his claim against the estate of his former partner Mr Jones. He had lived with Mr Jones and worked for him in his house and business for 'pocket money', relying on a promise that Mr Jones made that he would leave the house and business to him. Mr Jones did not keep his promise, but the court upheld Mr Wayling's claim on the basis of 'proprietary estoppel'.

Do you have a remedy against the solicitors who helped you buy the home?

If you bought the home jointly, or transferred it into your joint names, you ought to have been given sensible advice by the solicitors who dealt with the conveyancing, so that you knew the implications of what you were doing. The Court of Appeal (in the case of *Springette v Defoe*: see box) has said that it is probably negligent if the solicitor does not find out and record at the time of the conveyance what the joint purchasers' shares of the property are agreed to be.

If your solicitor failed to do this and you end up having to pay legal costs to establish your rights in the home, or you end up with a court case by which you lose part of the property, you may be able to recoup some of your loss from your original solicitor. You can explore the possibilities with your current solicitor, unless of course you are still using the same one. If this is the case, then you will need to take advice from another firm.

Death

Chapter 7 discussed what happens if your partner dies and you are not provided for properly. This chapter simply highlights what happens to your home if death rather than separation ends your partnership.

Is the home in your joint names?

If the home is in your joint names, how it passes on death depends on whether it is held as a joint tenancy or a tenancy in common, as outlined in the section on separation. If it is a joint tenancy, the home will come straight to you if your partner dies, and vice versa. If it is a tenancy in common, your respective shares will pass as provided for in your will; if you have no will, your share passes with the rest of your estate according to the 'intestacy rules', as shown on the chart at the end of Chapter 5.

Is the home in one person's name?

If the home is in your partner's sole name and he or she dies, the home will pass according to the will, if there is one; and if not, according to the intestacy rules shown in Chapter 5.

If this means that the whole of the home, or your partner's share in it, goes to someone else, then the Inheritance (Provision for Family and Dependants) Act 1975 provides you with a remedy. This circumstance is described in detail in Chapter 5. The court will have to apply the criteria laid down in that Act, but will bear in mind the principles, outlined under the section on separation, which would be significant factors in deciding issues between you if you were both still alive. In some cases the principle of 'proprietary estoppel' may gain you a share of the home.

A home that you rent

This section is intended to explain the rights that exist between you and your partner as tenants. (For much wider information on your rights as tenants generally, see *The Which? Guide to Renting and Letting*.) There is no power in the courts to order a transfer of tenancies between partners, except where there are children. If there are children the court does have powers, which it can exercise under the Children Act 1989, and these are described in the section on 'Capital orders for children' in Chapter 12. Your rights in the home (if you cannot take advantage of the Children Act provisions) depend on what sort of tenancy you have. There are different rules for private tenancies, council tenancies and housing association tenancies. These are dealt with separately below.

Private tenancies

There are different types of private tenancy, each with its own rules. Your tenancy will probably fall into one of the three main categories:

- an assured shorthold tenancy
- an assured tenancy
- a regulated or protected tenancy.

You need to check your tenancy agreement if you are not sure what type of tenancy you have:

- If your tenancy started on or after 28 February 1997, it is an assured shorthold tenancy unless the landlord has stated in writing that it is an assured tenancy.

- If it started between 15 January 1989 and 27 February 1997, it will be an assured shorthold tenancy if the landlord stated it to be so on a legal form when it first started. If he did not, then it is an assured tenancy.
- If your tenancy started before 15 January 1989, it will generally be a regulated or protected tenancy.

Tenancies can be either periodic or fixed-term. Periodic tenancies have no fixed end date when you sign the original agreement and simply continue from week to week, or month to month (depending on how you pay your rent), until either you or the landlord gives the appropriate notice. Fixed-term tenancies start off by being for a limited period: six months is typical. When an assured, fixed-term tenancy ends, if neither you nor the landlord has given notice, the tenancy continues as a periodic tenancy on the same terms as before. It then becomes a 'statutory periodic tenancy' and the landlord can bring it to an end only by getting a possession order from the court; simple notice to quit is no longer enough.

A tenancy in one person's sole name

The person who is the tenant has the right to stay in the property and can give the other notice to quit (which could be followed up by court proceedings) if the other does not go voluntarily. There is no statutory protection for the partner who is not the tenant.

If you decide, when you split up, that what you would both prefer is for the tenant to go and the other to stay, you will have to see whether you can negotiate with your landlord for the assignment of the tenancy to the other partner. However, you have no right to insist on this, so it will depend on goodwill from both of you, and your success will depend on your relationship with your landlord. You cannot compel your landlord to agree if you have an assured or an assured shorthold tenancy. Secure tenancies (see page 129) cannot generally be assigned at all.

A tenancy in your joint names

If you have a joint tenancy (of whatever kind) and one of you leaves the home, the other can continue to live there under the terms of the tenancy agreement. A fixed-term joint tenancy can only be ended by one tenant with the agreement of the other.

If you have a statutory periodic tenancy, or an assured periodic tenancy, there is a serious catch. Either of you can give the landlord notice to quit. This means, if you are the person staying in the property, that you are vulnerable to your ex-partner giving notice and effectively giving the landlord the power to evict you (although this is subject to challenge under the Human Rights Act). It may be better to approach the landlord immediately and see if you can negotiate the grant of a new tenancy to you alone, if you give notice to quit.

You are better off with a regulated or protected tenancy. If one joint tenant leaves, the other is entitled to remain in the home whether or not the one who has left gives notice to quit. Further, if you are the one staying put, you can give notice to quit, which will prevent the person who has left having the right to return and remain in the home as the statutory tenant.

The situation on death

Tenants' rights to succession are rather better after death. If you have a joint tenancy (of whatever kind), the survivor simply carries on with the tenancy and the tenancy continues under its existing terms. If the tenancy is in the sole name of the person who has died there are rights of 'succession', which depend on the type of tenancy it is (as described above).

Succession of a periodic assured tenancy, statutory periodic tenancy or assured shorthold tenancy

The tenancy automatically passes to the cohabitant if they were cohabiting before the death. This does not include a same-sex cohabitant, however (but this is subject to challenge under the Human Rights Act).

A tenancy can also be left by your will to your partner, so same-sex couples in this situation should make provision in their wills. However, if you have a periodic assured tenancy, your landlord can apply for possession of the tenancy if he does so within 12 months of the death of the original tenant. A fixed-term tenancy will simply come to its end at the period specified in the original agreement.

However, here there is an exception to the rules about succession. If the partner who has died had succeeded to the tenancy (by, say, inheriting it from his wife before the cohabitation started), then the tenancy cannot be passed on by a further succession.

Succession of a protected or regulated tenancy

The rules are slightly wider for the succession of a protected or regulated tenancy: it can pass to a cohabitant, or any member of the family who has lived with the tenant for at least two years before the death. In the 1999 case of *Fitzpatrick v Sterling Housing Association*, the House of Lords held that a close same-sex relationship could mean that although the survivor could not be treated as living with the deceased as 'husband and wife', he could be treated as being a member of the family.

A tenancy of this sort can pass through two successions, not just one, but a second successor must have been living with the first successor at the time of death and for a period of two years immediately before the death; he or she must also be a member not only of the first successor's family but also of the original tenant's family.

Council tenancies

You will normally have what is called a 'secure tenancy' if you rent your home from the council, unless you are in temporary housing or on an introductory tenancy.

If you are joint council tenants

If your partner leaves and you want to continue to have the benefit of the tenancy, you should make sure that you give notice to quit before your partner does as this will end your partner's interest, and you can then negotiate a new tenancy from the council in your sole name. If your partner has left and gives the notice first, you are vulnerable to possession proceedings.

If the tenancy is in one person's name

If the person with the tenancy leaves, the secure tenancy ends and the council can obtain possession. They can also grant a new tenancy to the person who has stayed. If you are obviously someone with a housing need, such as a mother with children, the likelihood is that you will get a new tenancy in your sole name.

If you are the sole tenant and your partner leaves, you simply continue with your tenancy.

What happens on death?

If you have a joint tenancy, the survivor simply continues with the tenancy. This counts as a 'succession' (see above), and the survivor will not then be able to pass the tenancy to a subsequent successor, as only one succession is allowed.

If the sole tenant dies then the tenancy can pass, by succession, to a cohabitant living as 'husband and wife', or a member of the tenant's family who has lived with the tenant throughout the period of 12 months ending with the tenant's death. A same-sex partner, following the case of *Fitzpatrick v Sterling Housing Association* (see above) should count as a member of the tenant's family.

You can also leave your tenancy by will, or it can pass to your next of kin if you have not left a will. Same-sex couples, so as to avoid any legal argument, should sensibly provide for the tenancy to pass to each other in their wills.

Housing association tenancies

There are a number of bodies such as housing associations, trusts and co-operatives that provide what is called 'social housing'. Tenancies with these bodies generally fall into the same categories as council housing or private tenancies, which are described above.

First, you have to find out what sort of tenancy you have.

- If your tenancy began before 15 January 1989, you probably have a secure tenancy, and the section above that deals with council tenancies will apply to you as well. Your tenancy may have started off with the council and then have been transferred to a housing association, or other body.
- If your tenancy began after 15 January 1989, it may be an assured, or an assured shorthold tenancy, as described above. You also need to find out whether it is for a fixed term (such as six months) or periodic (it runs from week to week or month to month). You will need to look at the agreement to find out, or check with the housing body itself.

Once you have worked out what sort of tenancy you have, look at the appropriate section earlier in this chapter to find out your rights if you separate, or your partner dies.

Chapter 15

Your interests in other property

Chapter 14 begins with a warning that there are no rules in law that give cohabitants the right to claim a home, unless it has been jointly held or treated as jointly held. This applies just as much to other items of property. This chapter looks at what lawyers still refer to as 'chattels' and other items of joint property such as bank accounts.

Here is another word of warning: few domestic assets have such value that you can justify the amount that you will spend in legal costs sorting out a dispute over them. It is often very hard to sort out the rights and wrongs over objects. You will run up an enormous legal bill and get yourself embroiled in a fruitless and bitter dispute with little prospect of getting what you really want out of it. It cannot be stressed enough that you will probably spend far more on lawyers than the value of the items, which is a terrible waste of money.

If you did not have an agreement about the things that you bought together and need to sort them out now, try to do it together. You can make a list of all the items and then try to sort out who should have what. You can decide how you want to do this. You may want to divide on the basis of the price that you paid for them, or you may want to look at their value now, rather than at the date of purchase. You may want to achieve a rough equality in the sorts of things that you have, so that one has the sitting room suite, and one the dining table and chairs, for instance. You can decide that the fairest way is to take it in turns to choose, or discuss items room by room. It really does not matter how you do it, providing you find a way of reaching an agreement. If you cannot do this without the help of someone else, this is a good thing to take to a mediation service.

The legal position

It is worth considering the strict legal position only if you cannot agree and the asset is so valuable that it is worth litigation. However, an outline of the legal position may help you to reach an agreement over who is entitled to what. Generally, these are the rules:

- If you bought something, and you alone paid for it, it belongs to you.
- If you bought something out of joint funds, without distinguishing in what shares you contributed, you own it jointly and equally.
- If you bought something and contributed unequally, then you own it in the shares in which you contributed to its purchase.

In most cases you will not be able to establish ownership by referring to documents. In the case of your home, the title deeds or the tenancy agreement will tell you who is the legal owner, but few assets have a legal document that tells you about this. A car may be registered in a person's name, but that is not conclusive proof of ownership; in the absence of a gift or a promise, the car would belong to the person who paid for it.

These rules can be upset by what you do or say to each other. If you buy something with your money but say to your partner, 'this belongs to both of us', or, 'this is yours' and behave as though you mean it, then a court can hold you to your promise. You can be regarded as having created 'a trust' of the property. You might do this consciously, as you do if you enter into a living together agreement. Or a court can find that you have created a trust by implication: your behaviour or what you have said led to the conclusion that the property should, for reasons of fairness, be shared or even transferred to your partner.

There does have to be a shared, or communicated, intention to share the property, however. Your partner cannot acquire rights in your property against your wishes. Imagine that you have an asset that your partner persists in treating as his or hers, although you have not said that you will share it, or behaved in such a way that that would be a reasonable implication. Your partner cannot simply acquire an interest in it by continuing to behave as though it belongs to him or her. (Many a man who has had his favourite jumper 'half-inched' in this way may smile ruefully at this.)

A 'trust' of a boat

Mr Prance, who was married, had a relationship with Mrs Rowe for 14 years from 1982. He several times said that he would leave his wife and set up home with her, but he never did. In 1994 Mr Prance bought a boat for them to live in, and Mrs Rowe gave up her house and put her furniture in storage. The boat was registered in Mr Prance's name, but he told Mrs Rowe that this was only because she had not got her Ocean Master's Certificate and he referred to the boat as 'ours'. When the relationship broke up Mrs Rowe claimed, and won, a half share of the boat.

Bank and other accounts

On the face of it, if you have a joint account with your partner, you hold it in equal shares and things that you buy from it are owned jointly and equally. But this is not always the case. If only one of you puts money into the account, although you can both draw on it, the strict legal construction would be that that money and any purchases made from it would belong to the person putting the money in. The strict legal position can be over-ridden by an agreement between you, or if your behaviour gave rise to a trust as described above.

The car

The legal position is that the person who buys the car owns it, even if it is registered in another's name. However, as already described, what you say and do can change this position. So if your partner buys a car, registers it in your name and tells you that it is yours, the implication would be that it has become your property.

Things that you owned before you got together

These will be your own individual property unless you have made gifts of them to each other. There could also be circumstances in which you have started to treat such items as belonging to you both and you have both contributed to their maintenance. For instance, before you met he had bought a classic car that was in need of restoration. You helped with the restoration, buying items for it and spending happy weekends covered in oil. He referred to the car as 'ours' rather than 'mine'. When you split up you could justify a claim to a share of the car on the basis that you had been led to believe that you had an interest in it and had acted to your detriment in helping restore it.

If you are still paying for things when you split up

If you have bought things using a credit card, credit agreement or loan, the person who made the credit agreement is liable for the repayments, as far as the lender is concerned. As described earlier in the book, you are jointly and severally liable if you took the loan out together.

The logical position ought to be that if you are paying for something, you ought to have it, unless you have said to your partner that you are buying the thing for him or her and, in effect, have already made a gift of it. If you were buying something jointly, you will have to decide between you who is going to go on making the payments and who will have the object. The credit company will not be bound by your decision that only one of you is going to be responsible for the payments, but it would be worth explaining to them the arrangement that you have made in any event, and telling them your new address(es). The reason for this is that if your partner says that he or she will take on the repayments and does not make them, the company can take debt recovery proceedings, and will name both of you. You do not have to be personally served with the proceedings; they can post them to your last address. You might find that a judgment had been obtained against you without your having had the chance to defend the proceedings. Judgments like this can affect your credit rating.

Chapter 16

Maintenance

There is no obligation in law for cohabitants to pay maintenance to each other. Only your children have maintenance rights. There is a popular belief that if you have lived together for a particular period of time (two years is often quoted), you get maintenance rights. In a survey by the National Centre for Social Research in 2001, nearly 40 per cent of those interviewed were under the impression that women did have rights to support after the breakdown of a relationship. This is not the case: there is no mechanism in the law for one former cohabitant to claim maintenance from the other for himself or herself, under any circumstances.

Attitudes are changing over this. Of the people questioned in the survey, 61 per cent thought that there should be maintenance rights, and the Solicitors Family Law Association★ and other bodies have made proposals for law reform. But there are no proposals for change on the statute book yet.

If you have children, you can get maintenance for them (see Chapter 12), but the court does not have the power to add on extra maintenance for you if you are the parent with whom they live. You cannot get maintenance 'by the back door' in this way. You could, however, make an agreement with your partner for a higher figure than you would normally have just for a child and ask the court to make this as a consent order.

The only way in which you could get maintenance would be if your former partner were prepared to pay it to you voluntarily. As there is no way in which you could compel him or her to make this payment, you would be relying on his or her generosity; or you might be able to agree it as part of a deal, in return for a share of capital that he or she would otherwise not be entitled to.

When you are thinking about what should go into such an agreement you need to include:

- clear details of the amount

Maintenance for mother by consent order

Paula and Harry split up when their son Tim was two. Paula had given up work when Tim was born, with Harry's agreement, as they felt that it would be best for him if she stayed at home while Tim was little. Paula planned to go back to work when Tim went to school.

They agreed that Harry would pay maintenance for Tim and that he would give Paula maintenance as well for the next three years. They agreed the terms of an order that the court was asked to make under the provisions of the Children Act. The maintenance was described as being for Tim. The order stated that it would run for three years at the higher figure and then would decrease to the lower figure.

In this way Paula had the security of a court order, which she could not have got if she had tried to make an application to the court against Harry.

- whether it is to be paid weekly or monthly or at another interval
- how it is to be paid (cheque/cash/standing order)
- whether it is to be paid in arrears or advance
- whether it is to be increased and if so by how much
- what events might cause it to end (death/marriage/another cohabitation).

If you are not specific, it can be hard to enforce an agreement, even if it has been made as a deed.

If you can make such an agreement, and record it in a legal deed, the agreement could be enforceable in a court, providing it has been properly drawn up. It would be enforceable not because of the maintenance element, but because of the form of the deed, which creates an enforceable contract between you. If you do decide to do this, then you need to take legal advice to get the agreement properly drawn up.

If you had a living together agreement that was drawn up as a deed and includes a promise to pay maintenance if you split up, then this too should be enforceable.

Chapter 17

Domestic violence

Violence and abuse in the home is remarkably common and affects all kinds of people and all kinds of relationships. It seems probable that, just as cohabiting relationships seem to be more fragile than marriages, so they may also be more prone to violence, and this seems to be true as far as children are concerned. Although there are of course thousands of kind and conscientious step-parents, it is a fact that children are more at risk from step-parents than they are from their own parents.

Where once domestic violence was scarcely classed as criminal, it is now taken far more seriously, particularly by the police. The political and social climate means that it is now actively condemned and campaigned against. However, it still goes on and it can be very hard to admit that it is happening to you, particularly if you consider your background and class not of 'that sort of people'. It can be still more difficult if you are male and the violence is being inflicted on you by your female partner, or if you are a same-sex couple.

However, the help is there. You can get swift remedies from the courts, if you need them, and there are many local agencies, refuges and support systems. Don't suffer in silence. As they say in the schools, 'Silence is the bully's friend.' Violence is never an acceptable or appropriate reaction, even if it is understandable. Many people who suffer violence from their partner feel that they are to blame for their partner's actions. They feel that they have nagged, or taunted, or in some other way provoked the violent act. We are all guilty of the wind-up, the angry word in the wrong place, the tactless observation, but we do not all get hit for it. If you are being hit, the violence to you is inexcusable, even if it is explicable. Take action. If you do not, and the violence is repeated, you may find it even more difficult to act to protect yourself. If you have children living with you it is even more important to take action. Children are harmed not only by violence inflicted on them, but also by seeing or being aware of violence in their home. Solicitors will often be told by their battered clients: 'I could cope when it was just me he was hitting, but when he started on the children I couldn't take it any more.' If those clients had taken action in the first place, the children would not have been hit at all.

You do not have to go as far as an injunction to protect yourself. You may feel that you want the relationship to continue, and that it can continue, if you can get rid of the violent element of it. There are a number of steps that you can take that fall short of an injunction. You can get a solicitor to write a letter pointing out that you could seek an injunction, and that this is what will happen if there is any repeat of the violence. You can find out if your police force has a domestic violence unit and talk to one of the officers there. She will be able to advise you what help the police can give you. They might be prepared to caution your partner, or simply arrest him or her – actions that fall short of a prosecution. She may know of anger management courses that your partner could take. Your doctor may also know about the availability of these as well. Experience in London suggests that the most effective remedy is to first approach the police for help. This is obviously cheaper, too, than instructing a solicitor.

If the violence is caused by drink you can seek help from Al-Anon, the section of Alcoholics Anonymous★ that helps friends and families of alcoholics. You may have other local services to help with drink or drugs addiction. The Citizens Advice Bureau should be able to tell you if there are any in your area.

It used to be a popular cliché to say that battered women enjoyed it and just went back for more. This is a gross over-simplification of the complicated emotional situations that people find themselves in. But it is true that even if you do get an injunction, it does not necessarily mean that your relationship has to end. What an injunction can do is redress the balance of power in your relationship and give you a new basis on which to proceed. Sometimes it can lead to a renewal of your relationship. More often, however, people do not seek an injunction unless and until they are sure that the relationship has no future and must be brought to an end.

Practical things you can do

Leave the home
From a tactical point of view it is probably a good idea to stay in your home if you can, but you may have to go for a short while to protect yourself and the children. If you do decide to go, take legal advice as soon as you can, so that you can protect your interests in the property if possible.

You may not be able to carry things like clothes or other necessities with you. However, if you contact the police, they will normally arrange to escort you back to the home later to collect some of your things in safety.

Get your injuries seen to

If you (or the children) have been injured, you will obviously need to get your injuries attended to. Try to get to your doctor as soon as possible so that you can be examined. If you are going to try to get an injunction a medical report will be very helpful, so tell your doctor that this is what you intend to do. Your solicitor can then contact the doctor to arrange this.

If your injuries are serious, you may have to go to the Accident and Emergency department of the hospital. Explain the same things to them. Try to make a note of the name of the person who treats you, so that you can tell your solicitor.

It can be very embarrassing to admit how your injuries have been caused, but do tell the doctor or the hospital the story, because they can refer to that in their report.

It will also be very helpful if you can photograph the injuries that you have suffered, if bruising or cuts are apparent. This is because, if you go to court, the marks may have faded. It sounds a bit ghoulish, but the judge will obviously be affected by how serious your injuries look, or looked. If you see a solicitor soon, she or he may have a camera and be able to take photographs. If you cannot see a solicitor immediately, you could use a photo-booth, or get a friend to take photographs, with a disposable camera if necessary.

Short-term housing

You may have a local women's refuge to which you could go. The police, or your solicitor, would be able to put you in touch with them. Women's Aid★ will also be able to give you advice. You will not find their addresses in the phone book, for security reasons, but their contact details are printed in the Addresses section at the back of this book.

Your local council should also be able to house you on a temporary basis if you have priority needs: if you have children with you, for example. The local housing department, or social services department, should be able to help you. The accommodation is not likely to be terribly salubrious; it will generally be what is called 'bed and breakfast' housing.

Legal remedies

The Family Law Act 1996 has 'tidied up' the law about injunctions. All the provisions that you need come within this Act and the injunctions that you can obtain can protect cohabitants, including same-sex couples. There are two kinds of protection order that you can obtain under the Family Law Act:

- a non-molestation order
- an occupation order.

These can be, and often are, combined.

Non-molestation order

A non-molestation order orders your partner not to assault, molest or otherwise interfere with you. This applies both to your partner's own actions and those of anyone acting for him or her. The order can also extend to protect your children (though generally the court will not add this to the order unless your partner has been violent in the past to the children, or threatened them with violence). Molestation includes any form of unpleasant harassment.

Cohabitants and former cohabitants can obtain non-molestation orders against each other. The Act lists several categories of relationship that come within its scope. These include people who live, or have lived, together as husband and wife, and people who live, or have lived, in the same household. The second definition includes (and this was the intention of the Act) same-sex couples.

Occupation order

An occupation order can order your partner to leave the home or use only part of it. Your partner can be ordered not to come within a certain distance of it, too. He or she can be ordered to let you come back into the home if you have left. You cannot use an order like this to obtain permanent possession of the home if it is in your joint names or your partner's sole name, but it will give you time to sort out the ownership in other legal proceedings.

When it comes to occupation orders, the Act makes a distinction between spouses and cohabitants, and a further distinction between male/female and same-sex couples. You have to know where you fit into the Act in order to make the correct application:

- If you are entitled to occupy the property – as an owner or co-owner, tenant or joint tenant – then you can apply under section 33 and it does not matter whether you are living as a male/female or same-sex couple.

- If you are not an owner or co-owner, tenant or joint tenant, but your partner is, and you are (or were) living as a male/female couple, then you apply under section 36.
- If neither of you is entitled to occupy the property (for example, if you were living in your parents' house) and you are (or were) living as a male/female couple, then you apply under section 38.

If you are one of a same-sex couple, and you have no legal entitlement to occupy the home (because you are not an owner or tenant), you are more vulnerable than a male/female cohabitant. You can get a non-molestation order, but you cannot get an occupation order to exclude your partner from the property in order to strengthen the protection.

The reason for making the distinction between the various sections under which you apply is that the court has to consider different factors under each section, as outlined below.

Section 33
Under section 33 the court must consider:

- the housing needs and housing resources of each of you and of any child living with you
- your financial resources
- the likely effect if an order is made, or not made, on the health, safety and well-being of both of you and of any child
- your conduct towards each other.

The court then has to apply what is called the 'balance of harm' test: it must make an order if it appears that the person applying for the order, or any child, is likely to suffer significant harm as a result of the behaviour of the respondent (the partner) if an order is not made; but the order should not be made if it appears that the respondent or any child is likely to suffer significant harm if the order is made, and the harm that they are likely to suffer is as great as, or greater than, the harm that the applicant would be likely to suffer if the order is not made.

Section 36
If you apply for an order under section 36 the court has to consider:

- the four factors set out above for section 33
- the nature of the relationship (and for cohabitants the court is specifically required to have regard to the fact that 'the parties have not given each other the commitment involved in marriage')
- the length of time that you have lived together as husband and wife
- whether you have any children or stepchildren

- the length of time since you separated (if you have)
- whether there are any pending proceedings about the ownership of the home or for support of the children.

The court should also consider a 'balance of harm' test as described for section 33, but the requirement that the court *must* make an order if the likelihood of harm to the applicant is greater does not apply to section 36 applications; the court can use its discretion.

Section 38
If you apply for an order under section 38 the court has to consider:

- the four factors set out above for section 33
- the 'balance of harm test' (described under section 33), about which it has a discretion.

Other orders that the court can make

If you get an order under section 33 or section 36, the court can also make other orders about:

- repair and maintenance of the home
- payment of the rent or mortgage or other outgoings
- use of the contents
- a requirement that reasonable care is taken of the contents.

How court proceedings work

You can apply to the family proceedings court (magistrates' court) or to the county court. Most solicitors will prefer to use the county court. Public funding is available for injunctions, if you are financially eligible. If your solicitors' firm has a public funding (legal aid) franchise they should be able to make a decision about whether an emergency funding application can be granted immediately. If you are seeking only a non-molestation order (this will be the case if yours is a same-sex couple: see above), there is a requirement that a letter should be sent to your partner asking him or her to stop harassing you and warning that an injunction can be obtained, before you get to the point of taking court proceedings.

You apply by filling in a long form (FL401). This should be accompanied by a sworn statement setting out what has happened between you and your partner. Once this is filed at the court, with the fee (currently £40; publicly funded clients do not have to pay), the court will fix a date for the hearing. The respondent (the person against whom the order is sought) must have two clear days' notice of the hearing and be served personally with the documents. Your solicitor should arrange all this.

If you need an order sooner than this, it is possible to go to the court without giving notice to your partner (this is called *ex parte*). You should take your solicitor's advice about whether this would be a good idea or not. It can generally be justified only where the violence has been extreme. In most cases it is not as useful as it seems. Courts will generally not grant orders that deal with the rights of occupation in your home on an *ex parte* basis, and any order that you get will be a short-term one, designed to protect you only until you come to court for the full hearing, on what is often called 'the return date'. Generally a return date will be fixed to take place in the next week or so, but this cannot be guaranteed.

On the day fixed for the hearing you will need to attend the court, and your solicitor should arrange with you where you will meet him or her or another person from the firm. If you have a barrister, you will probably meet him or her for the first time at court. You should make sure that you get there in good time, so that you can settle yourself down and talk to your lawyer(s). If your partner has been properly served with the papers, he or she should come to the hearing too. If your partner has been served and does not turn up, the judge can make orders anyway.

Your partner may well be advised by his lawyers to offer an 'undertaking' to the court. This is a promise not to molest you and, if appropriate, to vacate the home. This promise, if given to the court, is as binding upon your partner as a court order would be, and can be enforced. Many people would rather do this than have a court order made against them. If an undertaking is offered it will shorten the hearing, because there will generally not be any need to take evidence from both of you.

There is a problem with undertakings, however: the court cannot attach a power of arrest to them (see below). An order may be limited to a specific period, such as three months, or in very serious cases the court may decide to make it for an indefinite period.

Powers of arrest

If the court makes a non-molestation order or an occupation order it can attach a power of arrest to the order. This means that if your partner breaches the order, the police can be called to arrest him or her instantly, without the need for them to obtain a warrant, and he or she can be taken straight before the magistrates' court.

A power of arrest cannot be attached to an undertaking (see above). The court has to consider, therefore, whether the undertaking will offer you sufficient protection and the judge can refuse to take it, and instead hear the case and make an order.

If you get a power of arrest, your solicitors should make sure that the local police station immediately get a copy so that they are aware of it. You should be given a copy of the order in any event.

Breaches of the order

Once you have an order it is up to you to enforce it. There is no independent authority that will do this for you if your partner breaches it. You can enlist the help of the police if you have a power of arrest. If you do not have a power of arrest, you can still call the police if your partner is violent to you again. You can also take action in the civil court, where you originally got the order. You will need to take your solicitor's advice about the best course of action. You can apply to the court for your partner's committal to prison. The judge can send someone to prison for breach of the court order or of an undertaking. The sentence will depend on the seriousness of the breach. If the judge does not feel that the breach is serious enough to warrant a prison sentence, the injunction may be strengthened or renewed.

What to do if you are served with an injunction

If you know that you are at risk of being violent towards your partner, whether because you have been violent in the past or because you feel the tension in the home is becoming unbearable, you need to take steps to minimise the risk. Take responsible action, such as leaving the house for a cooling-off period.

If you are served with an injunction or injunction application, read it carefully, together with any other documents given to you, for example the sworn statement. See a solicitor as soon as possible and make an appointment with him or her as much in advance of the hearing date as you can. If you are financially eligible, you can get advice under the Legal Help scheme.

A few solicitors will not act for violent men, so check this in advance. The solicitor will take a statement from you and make this into a sworn statement to be lodged at the court. As an alternative to having an order made against you, you can offer the court an undertaking not to molest your partner. Breaking the terms of an undertaking can invoke just as serious a penalty as breaking the terms of a court order.

Unless you have real grounds to contest your partner's claim for a non-molestation order, you are unlikely to be able to obtain public funding to be represented in court, even if you would otherwise qualify on financial grounds.

Stalking: new court powers

Sometimes the stresses of separation can surface in obsessive behaviour from an ex-partner and stalking can be the result. The Protection from Harassment Act 1997, which creates a new criminal offence of what is in effect stalking, was brought into the law in June 1997, and gives courts extra powers for serious persistent harassment. Although stalking is not defined in the Act, it is well known as having come to mean open or unmistakable harassment, of which the victim is aware. The Act says that a person must not pursue a course of conduct:

- which amounts to harassment of another; and
- which he or she knows or ought to know amounts to harassment of the other.

Two criminal offences have been created by this Act (see box). The police can now take action to stop stalking and several cases have been brought against ex-partners. These include a 78-year-old man who stalked his ex-partner and her new lover, and a woman who bombarded her former lover with up to four abusive letters a day after he ended their relationship. (She also moved to a home two doors away from him and broke into his home wielding two carving knives.) The police can arrest someone who is stalking a victim. When the case comes to court, prison sentences can be ordered in very severe cases and the courts usually will order the stalker to cease having any contact whatsoever with the victim.

Stalking has also become, in lawyers' terms, a 'statutory civil tort', which means that a victim can claim money damages to compensate her (or him) for having been stalked, as long as a claim is made within six years of the conduct taking place. To try to avoid too much over-sophisticated legal argument about what the stalker intended, the new law says that these criminal offences are strict liability – that is, the victim's lawyer does not have to prove that the stalker himself or herself had criminal intent. The only defences are (a) prevention of crime; (b) legal authority (for example, where bailiffs have to enforce a judgment); or (c) that in the particular circumstances the conduct was reasonable.

Stalking offences

The Protection from Harassment Act 1997 creates two specific criminal offences:

- **the lesser**: causing harassment or distress (sections 1 and 2). A summary-only offence to be dealt with by the magistrates' court;
- **the greater**: putting the victim in fear of violence (section 4). This is 'indictable' which means it is likely to be heard in the Crown Court.

Part IV

Scotland and Northern Ireland

Chapter 18

Living together in Scotland

At present, cohabitants in Scotland do not enjoy the same legal rights as spouses. Family law in Scotland is an area which is due to be regulated by the Scottish Parliament rather than Westminster and, at the time of writing, proposals for reform are on the table. In September 2000 a White Paper on 'Parents and Children' was presented to the Scottish Parliament, and if the proposals within it are adopted and enacted they will radically reform many of the legal rules in respect of cohabitation for heterosexual couples. Nowhere in the proposals is 'cohabitation' defined, but the Scottish Executive has explicitly stated that this round of reforms will not place same-sex couples on an equal footing with heterosexual couples.

As well as identifying the similarities and differences between the laws of Scotland and those of England and Wales, this chapter also examines how the law in Scotland is likely to change during the life of the present Scottish Parliament, before the end of May 2003.

Matters covered by the same laws

Laws relating to state benefits, child support, Income Tax, Capital Gains Tax and Inheritance Tax are dealt with by UK-wide legislation and there are few differences, therefore, in the way these laws are applied in Scotland and in England and Wales. The consequences of living together as described in Chapter 8, State benefits, and Chapter 9, Tax, apply in much the same way in each country.

Although there are differences between Scots and English law regarding inheritance, such differences do not extend to the general rules of Inheritance Tax. The law reform proposals before the Scottish Parliament make some provision for cohabitants whose partners have died to claim a share out of the deceased partner's estate, but these proposals are unlikely to effect any changes to existing Inheritance Tax rules in Scotland.

Living together

Children

Parental rights and responsibilities

A child's mother has automatic rights and responsibilities in respect of a child, regardless of whether she is or has been married to the child's father. The position is more complex for fathers. At the time of writing, if the father was not married to the child's mother at the time of conception or at some later date, he will have *no* automatic parental rights and responsibilities in respect of the child. This is true even where the father has been named on the birth certificate and even where the child's parents jointly register the birth.

The Children (Scotland) Act 1995 clearly sets out the responsibilities and the rights that parents can have in respect of their children. Broadly, 'parental responsibilities' include the following:

- a duty to safeguard and promote the child's health, development and welfare
- a duty to provide the child with direction and guidance
- a duty, if the parent is not living with the child, to maintain personal relations and direct contact with the child
- a duty to act as the child's legal representative.

In Scotland 'parental rights' are distinguished from 'parental responsibilities'. Parental rights do, however, mirror the responsibilities outlined above and, in addition, include a right to have the child living with the parent or for the parent 'otherwise to regulate the child's residence'. These rights exist only to enable a parent to fulfil his or her responsibilities in respect of the child. Often, both parents have these responsibilities and rights in respect of a child. Because the old terms 'custody' and 'access' have become loaded with the implication of one parent holding all the cards, Scots law has moved away from these terms. It now refers to 'residence' and 'contact', which can, of course, be separated from the other rights and responsibilities that each parent may continue to hold.

Placing unmarried fathers in the same position as their partners

At the time of writing, there are three ways for an unmarried father to be placed in the same position as an unmarried mother in respect of their child:

- the parents marry
- the parents enter into a parental rights and responsibilities agreement

- an appropriate order is made by a court.

Marriage may not be an option for some couples. An agreement can be entered into only by consent. To go to court can be traumatic and costly. Oddly enough, despite the cost-effective and simple solution provided by a written agreement, not many couples have taken up this option. These agreements are in standard form and can be obtained from HMSO.* Although the signatures must be witnessed, there is no need for the parties to the agreement to have it formally sworn before a solicitor. In Scotland, these agreements must, if they are to be effective, be registered in a public register called the Books of Council & Session, at the Registers of Scotland.* A small fee will be charged for registration and for any additional copies that you require once registration has taken place.

Such an agreement places an unmarried father in precisely the same legal position as a married father with respect to parental rights and responsibilities. A couple entering into this type of agreement cannot pick and choose which rights or responsibilities he is to have.

It is important to be aware that these agreements can be entered into only by a child's natural parents. As in England and Wales any other partner of the mother can at present obtain parental rights and responsibilities only by way of court order, whether through the adoption process or otherwise. This is certainly a matter about which you should consult a solicitor.

Proposed changes

There is a strong possibility that much of the law in this area will be reformed by the end of May 2003. There is strong support in Scotland for the proposal that fathers who jointly register the birth of their child with the mother should have automatic parental rights and responsibilities along with the mother. There is also a view that step-parents, in particular, should be in a position to acquire parental rights and responsibilities by way of agreement with any other person who already holds those rights and responsibilities in respect of the child. However, it must be stressed that, on both counts, this is not yet the case.

Guardianship

For a variety of reasons, it is particularly important for unmarried couples to make wills. No distinction is made in Scotland for inheritance purposes between children whose parents are married and those who are not. Couples may, however, wish to ensure that guardianship of their child is dealt with in accordance with their wishes following death. The surest way to do this is to make appropriate provision in a will. In this, the law in Scotland differs from that in England and Wales. For example, in a situation where each of the parties living together holds parental rights and responsibilities, each party can nominate a guardian who will take on those rights and responsibilities in the event of death. In Scotland, should one of the parties die, his or her nominated guardian will hold parental rights and responsibilities *along with* the surviving parent.

It is therefore most important that couples think very carefully about whom to nominate, if anyone, as their child's guardian, as this person will share decisions in respect of the child with the surviving parent. It may also be worth restricting the circumstances in which the nominee is to become a guardian, for example in the event of the deaths of both parties.

This chapter simply highlights the differences between Scots and English law in these matters. For further practical considerations, refer to Chapter 4.

Inheritance

If couples living together choose to make wills and regularly update them, there should be no difficulty in ensuring that their wishes will be implemented on death. Be warned, however, that in the absence of a will:

- At the time of writing, Scots law makes *no* provision for a cohabitant to receive any share whatsoever in his or her partner's estate, as a cohabitant is neither a blood nor adoptive relative of his or her partner
- should your partner continue to be married to another person at the time of death, the law *will* continue to provide for the estranged spouse, regardless of how long the spouses have lived apart.

Remember that, even in Scotland, the term 'common law spouse' gives a person no special rights in relation to his or her partner. That it does is a myth which must be debunked. It is true that Scotland does continue to offer an ancient legal remedy called 'declarator of marriage by cohabitation with habit and repute', which allows a pursuer to establish that, to all intents and purposes, the couple considered themselves to be married and should benefit from the special rights that the law gives to spouses. However, successful cases are rare and extremely costly to pursue. Such court actions must be raised in the Court of Session, Scotland's highest court, and both solicitors and advocates must be employed. For these reasons it would be extremely unwise to rely on this doctrine's assisting in the event of a partner's untimely death.

Where a cohabitant dies intestate (without a will), his or her estate is subject to the set of rules laid down in the Succession (Scotland) Act 1964. These can be summarised as follows.

- Even an estranged spouse has automatic rights to inherit from the deceased spouse's estate in terms of 'prior rights' and 'legal rights'. Prior rights can include rights to a home, furniture and other household contents (sometimes referred to as 'plenishings') shared with the spouse.
- Children of a deceased parent also have legal rights to inherit from that parent's estate. Legal rights are restricted to rights in the 'moveable estate', which means, generally speaking, everything but land and buildings.
- 'Free estate' – that part of the estate left after prior rights and legal rights have been deducted – will usually transmit to the deceased's next of kin, in accordance with a table set out in the 1964 Act. Cohabitants do *not* appear on this table, nor are they considered next of kin for inheritance purposes.

At the time of writing there is no Scottish equivalent of the Inheritance (Provision for Family and Dependants) Act 1975, which enhances the rights of cohabitants in England and Wales to seek funds from the estate of their deceased partners.

Proposed changes

The law in this area is set for reform in Scotland by May 2003. At the time of writing the Scottish Executive is considering a proposal that will allow surviving partners to apply to the court within one year of their partner's death for a discretionary payment from the deceased's estate. This will radically alter the current position. Courts would, of course, be required to define the type of relationship which would qualify for this kind of award, and that may prove difficult. For the time being, the best advice is to have wills drawn up and re-examined at regular intervals.

Pensions and other financial matters

The law relating to pensions differs substantially between Scotland and England and Wales, particularly with regard to pensions as matrimonial property on divorce. These differences, however, relate almost exclusively to marriage and have no impact on cohabiting couples. The information in Chapter 6 is as relevant to those living together in Scotland as in England and Wales, as are the guidelines for protecting your position and that of your cohabiting partner. In essence, these are as follows.

- You should check with your pension scheme as to whether or not your death-in-service benefit will be paid to your partner on completion of the necessary nomination.
- If there is doubt that the trustees will use their discretion to fulfil your wishes, consider whether it would be better for your death-in-service benefit to form part of your estate.
- If your estate is to benefit, make a will, thus ensuring that your partner will benefit from your estate.
- Consider whether to nominate your children to receive your death-in-service benefit and provide for your partner, through your will, from the rest of your estate. This could be a more tax-efficient option.

Life insurance

As in England and Wales, life insurance policies can be written 'in trust', ensuring that the person nominated will receive the payment on your death. This is a safeguard worth considering. The payment bypasses your estate and is paid free of any potential Inheritance Tax.

In general terms, an insurance policy by one person on the life of the other will not be effective in the absence of an 'insurable interest' – that could be where one partner is financially dependent on the other's income, or where there is a joint mortgage or, in general, where the death of one partner would have a financial impact on the partner surviving. These days there is not usually a problem with heterosexual or lesbian cohabitants obtaining cover on the lives of their partners, but, as mentioned in Chapter 6, for gay male couples there can be difficulty in obtaining life cover.

Assigning a life insurance policy

If a cohabitant cannot obtain cover on the life of his or her partner, the alternative may be to take out a policy on his or her own life, with the benefits payable to the surviving partner and 'assigned' to that partner. This is done by executing a formal deed called an 'assignation'. On your death the person nominated (or 'assignee') will receive all the benefits due under the policy. Such assignations are commonly used with endowment insurance mortgages, the benefits being assigned to a bank or building society to ensure that any mortgage outstanding on the property you own at the time of your death will be repaid to the lender.

Even where a policy has been assigned to a lender, there may be additional sums due under the policy on your death (such as profits, terminal bonuses) which would have reverted to you on maturity of the policy. It is also possible to execute an assignation of these 'reversionary rights', thereby allowing the principal sum to be paid to the lender and any additional sums to be paid to your partner as the assignee.

Policies assigned in this way do not form part of your estate for Inheritance Tax purposes. A Deed of Assignation is required and the insurance company must be told about the assignation, by way of a formal 'intimation of assignation', before the assignation is legally effective. If this is what you intend to do, you should consult a solicitor in order to comply with the complexities of the procedure.

Contents insurance

Household contents insurance usually covers the possessions only of the policy holder and his or her family. 'Family' includes a spouse and children, but not necessarily a cohabitant. It would generally be necessary for a cohabitant to take out separate contents insurance cover or to become a joint policy holder with his or her partner. It is best to check the position with the insurance company directly.

Proposed changes

See 'Your interests in other property', later in this chapter, for proposed changes to the law that may affect financial property, particularly in the event of the breakdown of a relationship.

Being treated as next of kin

Medical treatment

The term 'next of kin' in Scotland has a legal definition when it comes to inheritance and distribution of the estate of the deceased, particularly where the person died without making a will. Matters are not quite so straightforward when it comes to medical treatment.

The situation in Scotland is much the same as that in England and Wales, as detailed in Chapter 7, particularly in relation to the attitude of medical practitioners. If you are able to advise those administering medical treatment as to your wishes, and are in a position to give consent to any medical treatment, there will be no problem.

Problems can arise, however, when you are not in a position to give such consent and your partner holds one view as to what would be best for you, while your blood relatives – perhaps your parents – hold another.

The Adults with Incapacity (Scotland) Act 2000 gives the same-sex partner of an incapacitated adult the status of 'nearest relative', provided the parties have lived together for not less than six months. This puts them on a par with heterosexual cohabitants. However, many medical practitioners are not aware of these provisions and time might be of the essence in dealing with medical emergencies. Having a document available for scrutiny could be more persuasive.

Another effective way of making provision for this situation is to prepare an *enduring* Power of Attorney, appointing your partner to act on your behalf in all matters relating to your welfare, including health matters. This type of Power of Attorney is often termed a 'Welfare Power of Attorney'. Although it can deal with many aspects of the welfare of an individual, it is subject to the overall provisions of the Adults with Incapacity (Scotland) Act 2000. There is little doubt that a cohabitant appointed as Attorney in terms of such a deed would find it easier to establish precedence over other non-appointed family members, as it would be the stated wish of the incapacitated partner.

Such a document must be drawn up by a solicitor and is subject to very strict rules. If you do wish to take advantage of such a provision, you should consult a solicitor.

Personal injury

While the law in Scotland recognises, to some extent, the status of cohabitants with regard to claims for damages in relation to personal injury or death, the legal provisions do not, as a matter of course, cover same-sex cohabiting partners. Under the Damages (Scotland) Act 1976 a partner can claim losses in respect of pain and suffering (known as *solatium*) from the wrongdoer for the other partner's death, but the law states that the claimant must be living with the deceased as 'husband and wife' immediately before death. Same-sex couples are therefore excluded from the scope of this statute. At the time of writing, the Scottish Law Commission is seeking views from members of the legal profession on whether this definition of partner should be expanded to include same-sex partners.

Under the Administration of Justice Act 1982, there is provision for a person who is injured to claim damages from the wrongdoer for the cost of necessary services (such as nursing care) provided by his or her cohabitant partner, and for the loss resulting from the inability to perform (as a result of injury) personal services for his or her cohabitant. Although these are similar provisions to those for spouses, where the court is quantifying such a damages claim it will look more closely at the stability of a cohabiting relationship than of a marriage. For same-sex cohabitants, the likelihood of an award being made is lessened.

Under the Criminal Injuries Compensation Scheme, a person who has been living with someone who dies as a victim of injury, for two years immediately prior to his or her death 'as if husband and wife', counts as a spouse for the purposes of claiming compensation. Same-sex couples are, therefore, excluded. A claim for special expenses under the scheme may be made where the injured person is cared for at home by a cohabitant partner, which could include a same-sex partner.

What changes if you marry

Throughout this chapter comparisons are drawn between spouses and cohabitants in respect of a number of different issues. If, as cohabitants, you decide to alter your legal status through marrying, you will automatically, as spouses, effect changes in your rights and your obligations in many of the areas discussed. As a spouse your rights will change in respect of inheritance, state benefits, pensions, occupancy of the matrimonial home, parental rights and responsibilities, and tax.

If the marriage ends

Distribution of property

If you have declared your commitment to a relationship by cohabiting, and subsequently decide to formalise this relationship through marriage, the last thing you may be contemplating is the effect such a step will have in the event of the breakdown of that relationship. Nevertheless, one of the fundamental differences between cohabitation and marriage is that, as soon as you become husband and wife, you automatically contract into the principles set out in the Family Law (Scotland) Act 1985. For the purposes of this chapter, the most important aspect of the 1985 Act is the way in which it deals with distribution of property on the breakdown of the marital relationship.

In terms of the 1985 Act, 'matrimonial property' is defined as property belonging to either party of the marriage, or jointly, which was acquired during the course of the marriage. For the purpose of the Act the 'course of the marriage' is taken to be the date of the marriage to the 'relevant date', which is generally the date the parties separated or, if they are still living together, the date when a writ for divorce is served on one or other of them. In terms of this definition, then, time spent cohabiting prior to marriage will not be taken into account as a matter of course when distribution of marital assets or the value of these assets is being dealt with. There are, however, exceptions to this general rule.

'Property' includes items such as interests in life policies, shareholdings, interests in private companies, businesses, partnerships, pensions and in essence anything that has a value which can be assessed. If, however, these assets are valued in relation to the period of marriage, the value of the property prior to marriage will not be taken into account. So, for example, contributions to an endowment policy in the name of one party will be valued only from the date of marriage to the date of separation, even if the policy has been running for many years prior to the date of marriage.

On the breakdown of marriage the rules of division of matrimonial property are fairly straightforward. The basic principle is that the 'net value of the matrimonial property shall be taken to be shared fairly between the parties to the marriage when it is shared equally or in such other proportions as are justified by special circumstances'. Equal division is the guiding principle.

In the context of division of matrimonial property, whether the property is held in the name of one or other spouse is irrelevant. Unless there are special circumstances, the spouses share equally in the value of all property acquired during the course of the marriage, regardless of who contributed to the purchase price. It really is a case of 'what's yours is mine, what's mine is yours'.

If an item is held in the name of one party, it is his or hers, but the separating or divorcing spouse is entitled to one half of the *value* of that property, even if they cannot claim one half of the property itself.

These rules with regard to equal division of property are in direct contrast to what can occur on the breakdown of a cohabitant relationship.

Debt
In the same way that the value of matrimonial assets is subject to a principle of equal division on separation, so too is matrimonial debt. The parties to a marriage are equally liable for debts incurred by either party during the course of the marriage. A wife cannot be forced by a third party to pay her husband's debts or *vice versa*, but the value of the matrimonial property to be divided will be the net value, that is total assets less total liabilities.

Other matters
The 1985 Act also gives courts power to issue incidental orders, and such orders can deal with the sale of property, the transfer of assets, etc. all within the context of an action for divorce.

Although a married couple may decide against court action on the breakdown of the relationship, and deal with division of assets through a negotiated settlement, the 1985 Act provides a framework for what is fair and reasonable within such a negotiated settlement. If a negotiated settlement is not fair and reasonable in terms of the Act, the disadvantaged spouse may be able to have it overturned at a later stage.

Often the threat of court action by one or other spouse will concentrate the couple's minds on reaching a negotiated settlement. Where no such persuasive deterrent is readily available, as in the case of cohabitation, the likelihood of reaching a negotiated settlement on the breakdown of the relationship is remote.

There is no doubt that the law provides safeguards, in relation to the distribution of property on the breakdown of the marital relationship, and can confer benefits on those who decide to undertake such a contract. But it also creates restrictions and obligations. Spouses have a duty to maintain or aliment each other for the duration of their marriage. A separated spouse can seek a court order for payment of aliment such as would not be available to a separated cohabitant.

Spouses cannot end their relationship by actions alone: walking out will not terminate the legal status of marriage. Only a court decree can do this, even if both parties consent to divorce.

On death, spouses cannot bequeath their property unrestrictedly; a surviving spouse will have automatic rights to claim on the deceased's estate.

Perhaps because of the restrictions and obligations imposed by entering upon marriage, many couples will choose cohabitation as their preferred legal status. Same-sex couples do not, under our present legal system, have the luxury of that choice. However, if couples choose not to marry, for whatever reason, they should nevertheless consider the legal implications of entering into their preferred type of committed relationship. This chapter seeks to outline some of those implications which should be addressed sooner rather than later.

Breaking up

Arrangements for the children

When relationships break down, the delicate balance of interests that was struck between parties who shared parental rights and responsibilities, or who behaved as such, can be one of the first casualties. Couples are strongly advised to resolve matters concerning the children by agreement – whether directly, through solicitors, or through mediation. As in England and Wales, there are several mediation services on offer, some of which are particularly skilled at dealing with matters concerning children. These services are coordinated by Family Mediation Scotland.*

A principle for all children
Regardless of whether a child is born to parents who are married or unmarried, any court required to make decisions in respect of a child must have the *welfare of the child* as its paramount consideration. In

Scotland this principle is enshrined in the Children (Scotland) Act 1995. Whilst there was a time when Scots law distinguished between children whose parents were married and those who were not, this is no longer the case.

Going to court

Court should be a last resort for couples, but if court action is taken the types of order which can be obtained include the following:

- an order depriving a person of (certain) parental responsibilities or rights
- an order imposing (certain) parental responsibilities or rights
- a residence order
- a contact order
- a specific issue order
- an interdict prohibiting certain steps being taken in relation to the child or his or her property
- an order regarding administration of a child's property by a third party
- an order appointing or removing a person as a guardian of a child.

These are known as 's.11 orders'. This refers to s.11 of the 1995 Act.

Procedure in Scotland does differ from procedure in England and Wales. First, a document called an 'initial writ' is prepared by the solicitor for the party seeking the order (the pursuer) and lodged with the appropriate fee at the relevant court. The writ is usually a fairly detailed document, setting out not only what the pursuer seeks but also the basis on which it is sought. The writ goes through a technical process called 'warranting' at court and is then returned to the pursuer's solicitor, so that it may be formally served on the party who opposes it (the defender). The defender's solicitor is likely then to lodge at court a NID (notice of intention to defend). This is a standard form which will have been sent out with the writ and which will be required to be completed by the defender. Once the NID is received by the court, a child welfare hearing is triggered. It may be some weeks before the hearing actually takes place and practice varies from court to court. The child welfare hearing may take place in the sheriff's chambers or in court but, in any event, no members of the public will generally be permitted to attend. A child welfare hearing is informal in nature. Neither the sheriff nor the solicitors present will wear wigs or gowns.

Scotland does not have court welfare officers. Instead, the sheriff will discuss matters directly with the parties and their solicitors, in the hope that some resolution can be achieved by way of discussion. The sheriff may decide that he or she requires to know more about the background of the case. He or she may call for a report to be prepared by a suitably qualified person, on the basis of discussion not only with the parents and relevant third parties but also with the children themselves. The views of the children will, generally speaking, remain confidential. It is, however, worth remembering that this can be a fairly traumatic process for the children involved.

A sheriff will make a court order only if he or she considers it necessary. It is preferred that parties reach consensus, even within the context of court proceedings. Usually any orders that are made are temporary in nature; these are called interim orders. As noted above, the welfare of the child must be the court's paramount consideration.

The sheriff may consider that further child welfare hearings are required, perhaps for the terms of a report to be considered by all concerned or to discuss a particular issue in depth. Only in the most contentious cases will a case ever come to proof. A proof is a hearing where witnesses are called, evidence given and final orders made. While there are cases where the parties are simply incapable of reaching agreement, remember that to take a matter to court is essentially to allow someone completely independent to make decisions in respect of your child. While you will have some input into the process, you will not have the final say. The decision may please neither parent. Agreement is often best.

Capital sums for children

In Scotland capital orders are not made in favour of children when their parents separate.

Child support

For the avoidance of doubt, it is worth noting that *all* absent parents, whether or not they have parental rights or responsibilities in respect of a child, have a continuing duty to maintain children under the age of 16, and children under the age of 18 who continue in full-time education. The legislation in respect of the Child Support Agency* (CSA) applies to the whole of the UK, and the information in Chapter 13 therefore applies to Scotland also. The CSA alone will generally deal with these cases. There is, however, an upper limit on the amount that a parent can be required to contribute by the CSA. If top-up sums for items such as school fees are required, court proceedings will be necessary to deal with these if agreement cannot be reached. Given that it costs nothing for the CSA to intervene, it is perhaps unfortunate that it cannot deal with all matters.

Your interests in the home

The legal systems in Scotland and in England and Wales have very different roots and nowhere is this more evident than in relation to the law of 'heritable' property. That said, the warnings contained within Chapter 14 regarding cohabitants apply equally in Scotland. As in England and Wales, there is presently no law giving cohabitants rights to share the value of each other's property in the event of separation. This contrasts sharply with the rules that apply in Scotland to married couples on separation.

A home that you own in your joint names

Property in the names of two or more parties can be held in different ways. The deed to your home should reveal precisely how title to your property is held. If the deed shows that the property has been disponed (given) to you and your partner 'jointly *and to survivor*', you and your partner's possession of the property will operate in much the same way as a 'joint tenancy' in England and Wales. This means that on the death of either party, the deceased's share will pass to the surviving partner, regardless of the terms of any will. This is the case regardless of whether the couple have subsequently separated. In Scots law this is called a 'survivorship destination'.

If the deed simply describes you and your partner as holding '*pro indiviso* shares', and the crucial words '*and to survivor*' are missing, then the property is held much like a 'tenancy in common' in England and Wales. That means that each of you has the right to dispose of your share as you wish in a will. In this case the shares may well be held in unequal proportions. If so, the deed will specify what these proportions are: for example, one quarter to X and three-quarters to Y. If the deed does not specify the proportions in which the shares are held, there is a presumption that the shares are held equally. In this case, on death, and should the deceased have no will, then his or her share will be dealt with according to the law of intestate succession, described above.

In neither of the above cases will a Scottish deed typically contain the English equivalent of a so-called declaration of trust, but there should be sufficient information to show precisely how the property is held.

Selling your share

In Scotland an owner of a share in a property cannot sell his or her share without the consent of the co-owner(s). If no agreement as to sale can be reached, he or she has the right to raise an action for division or sale. As always, the order sought is granted at the judge's discretion. Considerations such as the need to retain the house for a young family will be taken into account.

A home that you own in one person's name

A property held in the sole name of one party is just that. If you simply move into your partner's property or decide, for whatever reason, that title to a property which you and your partner purchase is to be held in the sole name of your partner, then there is a strong possibility that you will not share in the value of that property if the relationship ends. You may have contributed to the mortgage repayments; you may have carried out a number of improvements using your own skills or funds. You could still end up with nothing to show for the time, effort and money you have spent on your home.

In this situation, therefore, a contract between you and your partner setting out how the property is to be dealt with in the event of separation can be invaluable. If your relationship has broken down, goodwill is likely to be in short supply and agreement difficult to reach. You may each have your own version of conversations regarding future financial provision. Worse still, you may never have discussed it. If you find yourself in a disadvantaged position, your options are as follows.

You can seek a remedy in court. In Scotland the law of trusts is *not* generally applied to this situation. More often the ancient common-law doctrine of 'unjustified enrichment' may assist and a court action can be based on this.

It is usually a fairly straightforward matter to demonstrate to a court that one party has been enriched at the expense of another. It is not, however, at all simple to demonstrate that the enrichment has been 'unjust'. To do so, the wronged party must show that he or she has benefited the enriched party either:

- as a result of a fundamental error (e.g. making repayments to a mortgage which was wrongly believed to be held in joint names), or
- in contemplation of a particular circumstance (e.g. an unfulfilled expectation that the parties would one day marry).

In addition, the wronged party must demonstrate that he or she did not act mainly for his or her own benefit, that he or she did not intend simply to donate the funds, services or property in question to the defending party, and that there is no other legal remedy available. These are tough tests to meet and few cases have been successful. Rather than rely on such an uncertain remedy, it is strongly recommended that before contributing in any way to the running of a household, you consider and discuss the basis on which you are doing so and, where appropriate, formalise matters in a written agreement with your partner. This may seem unromantic but, as a cohabitant, you simply do not have recourse to the same legal remedies as a married couple.

Occupancy rights

If the title to the property is held in the name of your partner, he or she is 'entitled' and you are 'non-entitled'. Under Scots law the rights of non-entitled cohabitants to occupy the home are limited, but they are not non-existent. Under the Matrimonial Homes (Family Protection) (Scotland) Act 1981 (as amended), the non-entitled heterosexual partner of a cohabiting couple can apply to the court for a right to occupy the home. If the court is of the opinion that the couple were cohabiting in the house 'as if they were man and wife', it may grant occupancy rights to the non-entitled cohabitant for a period not exceeding six months. The wording of the Act therefore excludes same-sex couples, who cannot enjoy such rights, which include a right to enter the home and thus are of use even where the non-entitled cohabitant has been forced to leave. An application for occupancy rights should be made as soon after separation as possible. It is useful to note that the term 'house' includes any dwelling, including a caravan or houseboat.

Although occupancy rights can be granted only for a period not exceeding six months, at the end of the six-month period a further application to the court for renewal is possible. How often the court would renew the order is uncertain. Certainly, if there are children of the relationship living in the home, the court would take their welfare into account in considering whether or not to grant an order.

If the non-entitled partner has occupancy rights, he or she can also ask the court for orders granting use of furniture and plenishings within the home and for an exclusion order preventing the entitled partner from occupying the home.

Any occupancy rights of a non-entitled cohabitant will lapse on the entitled partner's death or on the sale of the property. In the latter case, it is possible for a non-entitled cohabitant who has been granted occupancy rights by the court to apply for an interdict prohibiting the entitled partner from selling the property while any occupancy rights subsist. If there is no such interdict and the house is sold, then the non-entitled cohabitant can claim damages following such a sale, but only while the court order granting occupancy rights remains in force.

Points to consider when purchasing a property

- Is the property to be held in one party's sole name or in the names of both parties?
- Are the contributions of each party to be reflected in the proportions in which the title is held? Note that the bank or building society will not be concerned about who owns what proportion of the property. Any loan will be made to both of you

and you will both be equally liable for repayments – that is, jointly and severally liable. If you think it would be fairer to reflect the difference in a contribution to the purchase price, and perhaps the difference in meeting the monthly mortgage repayments where one person is paying more than the other, this is best done by a separate agreement.

- If you intend to purchase the property jointly, do you want a survivorship destination in the title (see above)?
- Do you want a mechanism in place to deal with compulsory sale of the property in the event of the relationship breaking down? Again, this is best dealt with in a separate agreement.
- If the property is to be held in the name of one party only, then evidence regarding any understandings between the cohabitants regarding contributions to the purchase price, mortgage repayments and household expenses should be retained. In the event of a breakdown of the relationship this could be crucial in proving 'unjustified enrichment' or the existence of a constructive

---

A warning

Some court cases in Scotland since 1994 have highlighted the problems which can occur when a married couple, owning a property jointly, grant a Standard Security (the equivalent of a legal charge) to a lender as security for one spouse's (usually the husband's) business debts. In a number of cases the wife has argued that she signed the security under the undue influence of her husband or in ignorance of what it really meant. The efforts of the lender to repossess the property were, therefore, frustrated. In the case of *Royal Bank of Scotland plc v Etridge & Others*, a House of Lords decision in October 2001 laid down guidelines on the type of independent legal advice that a wife in such a situation should receive prior to granting such a security.

For the purposes of this book, it is particularly important to note that the comments of the leading Judge, Lord Nichols, suggested that his advice stretched beyond transactions involving married couples to unmarried and same-sex couples, if the lender is aware of the relationship. If, therefore, one partner takes out a loan, with a security over the house (for his or her own, not joint, purposes) the other partner should always be encouraged to seek independent legal advice on the consequences of granting such a security.

---

trust. Such a trust is an unwritten agreement that one partner holds a proportion of the property for the benefit of the other, regardless of what is in the title.

A home that you rent

If you rent a property together, and you are both named on the lease, you will have joint and several liability for all the obligations under the lease. Either one of you can be asked by the landlord to pay the whole of the rent.

If one of you moves into a property already rented by the other, the incoming partner will acquire no automatic rights under the lease and such a move could be in breach of the tenancy agreement, depending on its terms. Without a joint tenancy or the permission of the landlord, the incoming partner will have no legal protection against eviction.

Generally, there will be a provision within the tenancy agreement preventing the creation of a sub-tenancy, so that even paying rent to the original tenant will give the incoming partner no rights as a sub-tenant against the landlord.

Private tenancies

There are two main types of private tenancies:

- a tenancy entered into after 2 January 1989 will generally be an assured or short assured tenancy
- a tenancy entered into prior to 2 January 1989 will generally be a protected or regulated tenancy.

If the tenancy is in your joint names, regardless of whether it is regulated or protected, assured or short assured, you are both 'entitled' to live in the property. Either one of you can remain in the property even if the relationship ends and your partner leaves. Your right to remain will depend on when the tenancy agreement comes to an end and, at the end of the tenancy, on whether or not the law gives you a statutory right to remain.

Tenancy in one person's name: occupancy rights

If, as a cohabiting couple, you rent a property and the tenancy agreement is in the name of one partner, then under the terms of the lease that partner is 'entitled' to live in the property and the other partner is 'non-entitled'.

Although the 'non-entitled' partner has no rights under the lease, he or she does have a right, under the Matrimonial Homes (Family Protection) (Scotland) Act 1981 (as amended) to apply to the court for an order granting occupancy rights, as outlined earlier. For the purposes of the Act, a 'cohabiting couple' means a man and a woman who are living with each other as if they were man and wife, and therefore excludes same-sex partners.

The occupancy rights which the non-entitled partner can enjoy are exactly the same under a tenancy as under ownership: that is, if in occupation a right to continue to occupy the house, and if not in occupation a right to enter into and occupy the house together with any child residing with the cohabiting couple.

All of the rights that flow from an order granting occupancy rights as outlined above can be enjoyed by the cohabiting partner while the occupancy rights continue to exist, although it should be remembered that these will only be granted for a six-month period at a time.

Such rights to occupy stem from the other partner's status as 'entitled'. When that entitlement ends, such as by termination of the lease, the rights of the non-entitled partner will also end.

Tenancy in one person's name: transfer
Under the 1981 Act, on application by the non-entitled partner, the court can order the transfer of a tenancy, although the terms of the tenancy (such as duration) will not change on that transfer, except for arrears of rent for which the entitled partner will remain liable.

Succession in private tenancies
In a joint tenancy, as you are both entitled to live in the property, the death of a cohabiting partner will not affect the surviving partner's right to remain in the property. The surviving partner will simply assume all the responsibilities under the lease.

Where the tenancy is in the name of one partner only, however, matters are not so straightforward. The law does give some protection to the heterosexual cohabitant in the event of the death of the partner who was the named tenant in a lease. In the case of regulated, protected, assured and short assured tenancies, a person living with the deceased tenant 'as if they were husband and wife' can succeed to the tenancy of the home that they shared by virtue of their cohabitant status. For a same-sex cohabitant, much will depend on when the tenancy was entered into. The surviving partner in a same-sex relationship might be able to claim he or she was a member of the deceased tenant's family and, in a regulated or protected tenancy under the Rent (Scotland) Act 1984, be eligible to succeed to the tenancy. However, under the later Housing (Scotland) Act 1988, which governs private tenancies entered into after 2 January 1989, same-sex cohabitants under a lease entered into after 2 January 1989 are unlikely to be able to succeed to a tenancy of their predeceasing partner, as they were not living together 'as husband and wife' and this Act makes no provision for succession by 'family'.

It is likely that the law in this area will change in the near future for same-sex cohabitants, as pressure is being exerted to eradicate this type of discrimination. Until it is, however, joint tenancies in private sector leases might be the wisest choice.

The law relating to tenancies is extremely complex, and if you are in any doubt as to your rights in a tenancy under the relevant legislation, you should consult a solicitor or local Citizens Advice Bureau.

Public-sector tenancies

In public-sector tenancies (where the landlord is a local authority or housing association) where the cohabiting couple rent the property jointly, the rules are fundamentally the same as for private sector housing: you are jointly and severally liable for the obligations under the lease and if one party leaves, the other has a right to remain.

Problems can arise, however, where the tenancy is in the name of one partner only. If the named tenant leaves the property, or 'abandons' it, the remaining partner can apply to the local authority for the tenancy. Whether or not this will be granted will be at the discretion of the authority as landlord. It will take a variety of matters into consideration, including the length of time for which the cohabitation relationship has existed, whether or not children of the relationship are living with the resident partner, and whether or not the remaining partner occupies the property as his or her only or principal home. It can be difficult for the remaining partner to prove cohabitation, and each authority will have its own guidelines with regard to the length of the relationship required, etc. There is no doubt that it is easier for a spouse who remains in such a property to acquire the tenancy. If you are in any doubt as to your status under a public-sector tenancy, contact your local authority or housing association.

Succession in public-sector tenancies

On the death of a tenant in a public-sector tenancy, the tenancy will pass by law to 'a qualified person'. The law previously defined a 'qualified person' as someone who was living in the property as his or her principal home at the time of the tenant's death and was either the tenant's spouse or living with the tenant as 'husband and wife'. The Housing (Scotland) Act 2001, dealing with public-sector housing, has amended this definition to include cohabitants in a same-sex relationship, if the couple had been living together for six months prior to the death of the predeceasing partner.

The position of same-sex couples with regard to public-sector tenancies, therefore, has improved. Nevertheless, it would be wise to take any tenancy in joint names if possible.

Your interests in other property

In Scots law property that is not 'heritable' is classed as 'moveable'. The presumption of equal ownership in household goods and in property derived from a housekeeping allowance that flows from the status of marriage does not apply to cohabitants. The only way in which the cohabitant owner can be deprived of the use of his or her property is where an order for use of furniture and house contents has been granted by the court to a non-entitled partner enjoying occupancy rights, as outlined earlier.

The rule, then, is simple: the partner who paid for the goods is the owner of those goods and will remain so, unless there is clear evidence of a gift from one to the other or sufficient evidence to show that the intention of both parties was that ownership would pass from one to the other. If a gift is made to a cohabiting couple, ownership will depend on whether the person making the gift intended it for one or other of the cohabitants. In the absence of such evidence there is a presumption that the property is owned in common, each partner being entitled to one half either of the item or of the value of the item.

Proposed changes

Proposed reforms in Scots law for cohabitants would lead to changes in this respect, as follows.

- There would be a presumption that cohabitants have equal shares in household goods, regardless of who purchased the goods, or who has the main use of them. This presumption will apply only to goods acquired during the period of cohabitation and not to goods bought in prospect of cohabitation. The presumption can be disproved if it can be shown that the goods belong to one party alone or to both in unequal shares.
- There will be a presumption of equal shares in money and property that derives from a housekeeping or similar allowance. Therefore where one partner is the sole breadwinner, the non-earning partner will have an equal right to any property purchased through an allowance or to savings made from that allowance. For the cohabiting partner who stays at home to bring up the children,

for example, this could make a substantial difference to the success of any claim for a share of property or financial products on the breakdown of the relationship.

- There are no proposals for equal liability for debt, and in general cohabitants will continue to be liable for debts in their own name only – unless of course they are jointly and severally liable, for example under a hire purchase agreement, a mortgage or an overdraft on joint accounts. In addition, couples living together will continue to be jointly and severally liable for council tax due for the period during which they lived together. Credit-card debts, etc., will continue to be the liability of the individual card holder unless, of course, there is a credit-card account in joint names.

Remember that these reforms have not yet been implemented.

Aliment (Maintenance)

As in England and Wales, a cohabitant presently has no right to aliment from a partner. The Child Support Act, in fixing the amount of maintenance payable by an absent parent for the child, is effectively supporting the parent with whom the child is residing.

Capital provision
At the time of writing, there is no right in Scots law to financial provision for a cohabitant on dissolution of the relationship. However, the proposals for financial provision in the White Paper currently awaiting enactment by the Scottish Executive will allow a former cohabitant, on the breakdown of the relationship, to apply to a court for some financial provision, within one year from the end of the cohabitation. As well as having the power to award a capital sum (including a capital sum payable by instalments) where appropriate, the court will also have the power to make an interim award. Such an interim award would be the equivalent of aliment pending payment of the capital sum.

Domestic violence

As a cohabitant who is facing abuse at the hands of a partner, you should have no hesitation in requesting immediate assistance from the police. Should it be necessary, however, to obtain orders from court with a view to deterring future abuse, some thought must be given to how best to do so. A patchwork of remedies is available, which, broadly speaking, fall into three categories:

- common-law orders interdicting specific behaviour

- orders under the Matrimonial Homes (Family Protection) (Scotland) Act 1981(as amended)
- orders under the Protection from Harassment Act 1997.

Common-law orders

These orders are not governed by any particular statute. In Scotland, they are called interdicts, not injunctions. An interdict is an order which prohibits specific behaviour. The interdict must state exactly the type of behaviour which is prohibited, e.g. 'placing X in a state of fear, alarm or distress'. An order that simply attempts to restrict civil liberties, e.g. 'interdicting Y from entering the boundaries of the city of Aberdeen' will not be granted.

These orders can be granted against any individual; you do not have to have a special relationship with that person. For this reason, they are a particularly attractive option for cohabitants, whether in a heterosexual or a same-sex relationship.

Until very recently powers of arrest could not be attached to common-law interdicts. This was considered to be a major drawback. The Protection from Abuse (Scotland) Act 2001 came into force on 6 February 2002, however, from which date powers of arrest could be attached, if sought, to common-law interdicts. The applicant must specify when the power of arrest is to expire, being a date no later than three years after the date on which the power of arrest is granted. Thereafter, the duration of the power of arrest can be extended only by further application to the court.

Orders under MH(FP)(S)A 1981

Orders under this statute can prohibit or restrain the conduct of one spouse towards the other spouse or a child of the family, or prohibit a spouse from entering or remaining in a matrimonial home or in a specified area in the vicinity of the matrimonial home. Although the word 'spouse' is used here, this statute also applies to parties who are living together 'as man and wife'. In short, this legislation can be used by cohabitants who are in a heterosexual relationship. If you are in a same-sex relationship, however, these orders cannot be invoked by you.

Typically, these orders fall into two categories: interdicts and exclusion orders. The nature of interdicts is discussed above, while exclusion orders suspend the occupancy rights of one party in the family home. A court must make the order: 'if it appears to the court that the making of the order is necessary for the protection of the applicant or any child of the family from any conduct or threatened or reasonably apprehended conduct of the non-applicant spouse which is or would be injurious to the physical or mental health of the applicant or child' (s.4 (2)).

Powers of arrest can be attached to orders granted under this Act.

Orders under the Protection from Harassment Act 1997

Like common-law interdicts, orders under this Act can be made against any individual. There is no need for the applicant to have any special relationship with the person whose behaviour is in question. A party in a heterosexual or same-sex relationship can seek an order under this Act.

The basic premise of the Act is that: 'a person must not pursue a course of conduct which amounts to harassment of another and (a) is intended as harassment or (b) occurs in circumstances where it would appear to a reasonable person that it would amount to harassment of that person' (s.8 (4)a).

The Act can be invoked only where the behaviour in question has occurred on at least two occasions. Different types of order can be granted in terms of this Act, including non-harassment orders and interdicts.

Additionally, in terms of this Act the applicant may obtain damages for the anxiety caused by the harassment and for any financial loss which has resulted from it.

Which remedy is best?

It is worth seeking advice from a solicitor on the best remedy for your particular problem and in your particular circumstances. In most cases, one of the above remedies must be chosen, as two cannot run together.

Chapter 19

Living together in Northern Ireland

Northern Ireland is a separate legal jurisdiction within the UK, with its own laws and procedures. While to a large extent the law in Northern Ireland closely mirrors that in England and Wales, there are certain differences. The most important – though not all – of these are highlighted in this chapter.

Getting together

Setting up home together

Northern Ireland's property laws are based on Irish rather than English land law. However, the advice given in Chapter 1 of this book is very relevant to those setting up home in Northern Ireland.

In Northern Ireland local councils are not the providers of public housing. This is the responsibility of the Northern Ireland Housing Executive.* Advice should be sought from their local offices if your partner intends to move into your rented home.

Other joint arrangements

Council tax and water rates do not apply in Northern Ireland. Instead, taxation is levied by way of domestic rates, which comprise an element of taxation by central government and an element of taxation by local councils. Rates are calculated using a district rate (set by the local council) and a regional rate (set by central government) and are then determined based on the size of your property. Rates can be in the joint names of you and your partner and as such you will be jointly and severally liable.

Living together

Children

Northern Ireland's equivalent of the Children Act 1989 is the Children (NI) Order 1995. This brought Northern Ireland's legislation largely into line with England and Wales.

In Northern Ireland, as in England and Wales, parental responsibility is not an automatic right conferred on an unmarried father. An unmarried father can get parental responsibility in the same way as in England and Wales. In addition, the Family Law Act (NI) 2001 will ensure that an unmarried father whose name appears on the child's birth certificate automatically acquires parental responsibility.

There is a particular parental responsibility agreement form for use in Northern Ireland. Solicitors who specialise in children's law should have these forms available and should be able to assist in having them properly completed and filed. A list of these solicitors is available from the Law Society of Northern Ireland.* Essentially the procedure for completing a parental responsibility agreement form is the same as in England and Wales. Once the form has been signed by both the mother and father and proper evidence of identity has been produced, the agreement must be filed in the Office of Care & Protection* based in the Royal Courts of Justice, Belfast.

The responsibility for registering a child's birth in Northern Ireland is that of the mother. The birth must be registered within six weeks of the child being born.

In Northern Ireland the equivalent of the Inheritance (Provision for Family and Dependants) Act 1975 is the Inheritance (Provision for Family and Dependants) Order 1979. Like its English and Welsh equivalent, this empowers the dependant to apply for reasonable provision out of a deceased's estate.

Inheritance

The intestacy table which shows where property will go if you die without making a will in Northern Ireland is on pages 176 and 177. These financial limits do change from time to time. Therefore the advice given in Chapter 5, to make a will, is equally valid in Northern Ireland.

In Northern Ireland public funding is still known as the 'green form scheme'. Many solicitors will be prepared to draw up a will using this scheme. The criteria for obtaining public funding in Northern Ireland differ from those in England and Wales. A solicitor should be able to advise on whether you might be eligible.

Enduring Powers of Attorney are used widely in Northern Ireland. Again, the form itself differs from that used in England and Wales. If the power needs to be registered, this is done by way of an application to the Master of the Office of Care & Protection* based in the Royal Courts of Justice in Belfast. The Master can authorise the attorney to continue to act on a person's behalf once that person has become incapable of managing his or her own affairs.

If you are left without provision following the death of your partner, a claim can be made under the Inheritance (Provision for Family and Dependants) Order 1979, which is Northern Ireland's equivalent of the Inheritance (Provision for Family and Dependants) Act 1975. The Northern Ireland legislation largely mirrors that which applies in England and Wales.

Breaking up

Mediation
Like England and Wales, Northern Ireland is slowly coming to realise the value of mediation in resolving disputes, particularly those of a family nature. The Law Society of Northern Ireland★ has now established a panel of mediators who can offer mediation in a variety of disputes. To appoint a mediator from the Law Society's panel you should contact the Law Society and ask for an application form.

Arrangements for the children
Northern Ireland's equivalent of the Children Act 1989, the Children (NI) Order 1995, approaches the issues of separating couples in the same way as that in England and Wales. The courts in Northern Ireland will regularly make orders in respect of residence, contact and specific issues. Again, as special procedures apply in Northern Ireland, advice from those specialising in this area should be sought. For those on low incomes, Legal Aid may be available to assist in funding a case.

Child support
In Northern Ireland there is an absolute obligation on a parent to maintain a child. A parent can make application to the Child Support Agency★ (CSA) to obtain child maintenance from an absent parent.

If an unmarried father seeks to deny paternity, a CSA assessment can still be made, as an application can be made to the court for a declaration of parentage. DNA is the recognised method of determining paternity, although the court can direct blood tests.

Your interests in the home
Many cohabitants in Northern Ireland are surprised to discover that simply living together is not sufficient to create a legal interest in the property which they share (either rented or owned). Cohabitants who are splitting up must have recourse to basic principles of land law and equity. They do not have the same rights as married couples, who can ask a court to exercise a range of property adjustment powers. Where

Table of Distribution for Deaths on or after January 1 1956

The following is a quick reference table illustrating distribution in the most common situations of intestacy.

SPOUSE SURVIVING

Relatives surviving in addition to spouse	*Entitlement*
Issue	The spouse gets the personal chattels, and the first £125,000 absolutely. If there is only one child the spouse takes one-half of the residue and the child the other half. If there are two or more children, the spouse takes one-third of the residue, and the children divide the other two-thirds between themselves. Children who have pre-deceased the intestate leaving surviving issue of their own are represented by those issue. Parents and siblings receive nothing.
Parents (no issue)	The spouse is entitled to personal chattels and the first £200,000 absolutely. The spouse is also entitled to one-half of the residue. The remaining one-half residue is divided equally between the parents, if both alive, or given entirely to the sole parent.
Siblings	The situation is the same as that concerning the parents above, only the remaining half residue is divided between the siblings and if any siblings have pre-deceased the intestate leaving issue, then those issue take the share to which their parent would have been entitled.
No issue, no parent no sibling (or issue)	In this case spouse takes everything absolutely.

Source: Gratton, *Succession Law in Northern Ireland*, SLS Legal Publications (NI)

NO SURVIVING SPOUSE

Relatives surviving	*Entitlement*
Issue	The issue take *"per stirpes"*.
Parents	If two surviving, entitled to estate in equal shares, or if only one, the whole estate absolutely.
Siblings (whole or half-blood)	The whole estate in equal shares. Issue of a deceased brother or sister take their parents' share by representation.
Grandparents	If only one surviving, the whole estate absolutely. If more than one, the whole estate in equal shares.
Uncles and aunts	The whole estate in equal shares. Issue of a deceased uncle or aunt take their parents' share by representation.

If there is more than one person of the same degree, the assets are distributed equally. In the case of siblings and uncles and aunts, the surviving issue of the siblings or uncles and aunts who have pre-deceased the intestate take *per stirpes* the share that that sibling, uncle or aunt would have taken if he or she had survived the intestate. None of the later categories are represented by issue.

If the situation is not covered by any of the cases listed above, the 'pecking order' to determine the next-of-kin continues as follows:

great-grandparents;

grand-uncles and aunts;

great-great-grandparents;

great-grand-uncles and great-grand aunts and children of grand-uncles and grand-aunts (these categories are both of the same degree);

great-great-great-grandparents;

second cousins (ie, children of the children of grand-uncles and grand-aunts or children of great-grand-uncles or great-grand-aunts);

other next-of-kin of the nearest degree.

In the absence of next-of-kin, the estate passes to the Crown as *bona vacantia*.

cohabitants reside in property which is in the joint names of a person and his or her spouse, either spouse may make application to the court for a declaration as to the legal and proprietary rights in the property. The cohabiting parties' interest can only be declared by the court where the cohabitant has been served with the proceedings. The powers of the court upon making such a declaration are confined to ordering the division or sale of the property.

Maintenance

In Northern Ireland cohabitants do not enjoy any entitlement to maintenance. The law in Northern Ireland does not make any provision for what is commonly called palimony.

Domestic violence

The Family Homes and Domestic Violence (NI) Order 1998 allows a court to make orders between 'associated persons'. The term 'associated persons' includes cohabitants or former cohabitants. Therefore where there has been any form of harassment between cohabitants or former cohabitants, the court can choose from a menu of orders in an attempt to provide the applicant with some relief. These orders can include an occupation order, which has the effect of allowing one partner to reside in the home while the other must leave, or a non-molestation order, which makes any further form of harassment between the partners a criminal offence.

Addresses

Alcoholics Anonymous
Head office, tel: (01904) 644026
London helpline, tel: 020-7833 0022
Website:
www.alcoholics-anonymous.org.uk

Asian Family Counselling Service
Suite 51, The Lodge
Windmill Place
2–4 Windmill Lane
Southall
Middlesex UB2 4NJ
Tel/Fax: 020-8571 3933
Email: afcs99@hotmail.com

Association for Shared Parenting
PO Box 2000
Dudley
West Midlands DY1 1YZ
Tel: (01789) 751157
Volunteer line: (01789) 750891
(evenings only)
Website:
www.sharedparenting.org.uk

Association of Consulting Actuaries
1 Wardrobe Place
London EC4V 5AG
Tel: 020-7248 3163
Fax: 020-7236 1889
Email: acahelp@aca.org.uk
Website: www.aca.org.uk

Bar Council
Complaints Department
Northumberland House
303-306 High Holborn
London WC1V 7JZ
Tel: 020-7440 4000

(for advice and a complaints form)
or
3 Bedford Row
London WC1R 4DB
Tel: 020-7242 0082 *(for advice and to
obtain publications/leaflets)*
Fax: 020-7831 9217
Website: www.barcouncil.org.uk

Bar Council's Pro-Bono Unit
7 Grays Inn Square
London WC1R 5AZ
Tel: 020-7831 9711
Fax: 020-7831 9733
Web: www.barprobono.org.uk
Email: enquiries@
barprobonounit.f9.co.uk
Applications for assistance in writing only

Both Parents Forever
39 Cloonmore Avenue
Orpington
Kent BR6 9LE
Tel: (01689) 854343
*Provides help and advice to all parents and
grandparents involved in separation,
divorce or care proceedings*

**British Agencies for Adoption and
Fostering (BAAF)**
Skyline House
200 Union Street
London SE1 0LX
Tel: 020-7593 2000
Fax: 020-7593 2001
Email: mail@baaf.org.uk
Website: www.baaf.org.uk

British Association of Lawyer Mediators (BALM)
The Shooting Lodge
Guildford Road, Sutton Green
Guildford
Surrey GU4 7PZ
Tel: (01483) 236237
Fax: (01483) 237004
Website: www.balm.org.uk

Cambridge Family and Divorce Centre
Essex House
71 Regent Street
Cambridge CB2 1AB
Tel: (01223) 576308
Fax: (01223) 576309
Email: contact@cfadc.freeserve.co.uk

Child Abduction Unit
Official Solicitor's Department
4th floor
81 Chancery Lane
London WC2A 1DD
Tel: 020-7911 7045/7047
Fax: 020-7911 7248

Childline
Helpline, tel: (0800) 1111
Website: www.childline.org.uk
A confidential listening and advisory service

Child Poverty Action Group
94 White Lion Street
London N1 9PF
Tel: 020-7837 7979
Fax: 020-7837 6414
Website: www.cpag.org.uk

Children's Legal Centre
University of Essex
Wivenhoe Park
Colchester
Essex CO4 3SQ
Helpline, tel: (01206) 873820
(weekdays 10-12, 2-4.30)
Fax: (01206) 874026
Website: www2.essex.ac.uk/clc;
www.childrenslegalcentre.com
Email: clc@essex.ac.uk

National organisation aiming to improve the law and policy affecting children in England and Wales. Advice for children with legal problems; service also available for adults

Child Support Agency
Enquiry line, tel: (0845) 713 3133
Website: www.dwp.gov.uk

Community Legal Service
Directory line: (0845) 608 1122
Website: www.justask.org.uk

Comprehensive Acredited Lawyer Mediators
Caroline Graham
MacLeod & MacCallum
28 Queens Gate
Inverness IV1 1YN
Tel: (01463) 239393
Fax: (01463) 222879
Email: mail@macandmac.co.uk

Council of Mortgage Lenders
3 Savile Row
London W1F 3PB
Information line: 020-7440 2255
Web: www.cml.org.uk
Provides a useful free factsheet called 'Assistance with Mortgage Payments'

Couple Counselling Scotland
40 North Castle Street
Edinburgh EH2 3BN
Tel: 0131-225 5006
Fax: 0131-220 0639
Email: enquiries@
couplecounselling.org
Website: www.couplecounselling.org

Dawn Project
South Yorkshire Surviving
Separation and Divorce
95-99 Effingham Street
Rotherham S65 1BL
Tel: (01709) 309130
Fax: (01709) 512550
Email: dawn@dawnproject.
u-net.com

Department of Health (adoption)
Website: www.doh.gov.uk/adoption

Department of Work and Pensions (DWP)
Public enquiry office
Tel: 020-7712 2171
Fax: 020-7712 2386
Website: www.dwp.gov.uk
For general enquiries contact your Benefits local office

Disability Working Allowance Unit
The Inland Revenue
PO Box 178
Preston PR1 0YY
Tel: (0845) 605 5858
Fax: (0845) 608 8844
Minicom: (08456) 088844

Divorce Registry
First Avenue House
42–49 High Holborn
London WC1V 6NP
Tel: 020-7947 6000

Families Need Fathers
134 Curtain Road
London EC2A 3AR
Tel: 020-7613 5060
Website: www.fnf.org.uk

Family Credit Unit
Tel: (01253) 500050

Family Mediation Scotland
127 Rose Street
South Lane
Edinburgh EH2 4BB
Tel: 0131-220 1610
Fax: 0131-220 6895
Email: info@
familymediationscotland.org.uk
Website:
www.familymediationscotland.
org.uk

Family Records Centre
Public Search Room
1 Myddelton Street
London EC1R 1UW
(personal visits only)
Recorded information line:
(0870) 243 7788
Certificate enquiries, tel: (0870) 243 7788
General enquiries, tel: 020-8392 5300
Fax: 020-8392 5307
Website: www.pro.gov.uk

Family Welfare Association
501–505 Kingsland Road
London E8 4AU
Tel: 020-7254 6251
Fax: 020-7249 5443
Email: fwa.headoffice@fwa.org.uk
Website: www.fwa.org.uk

Grandparents Federation
Moot House
The Stow
Harlow
Essex CM20 3AG
Advice line: (01279) 444964
(weekdays)
Office: (01279) 428040
Email: info@talk21.com
Website:
www.grandparents-federation.org.uk

HMSO
St Clements House
2–16 Colegate
Norwich NR3 1BQ
Tel: (01603) 621000
Website: www.hmso.gov.uk

Institute of Legal Executives
Kempston Manor
Kempston
Bedford MK42 7AB
Tel: (01234) 841000
Fax: (01234) 840373
Email: info@ilex.org.uk
Website: www.ilex.org.uk

Land Charges Department
Plumer House
Crownhill
Plymouth PL6 5HY
Tel: (01752) 636666
Fax: (01752) 636699

HM Land Registry
32 Lincoln's Inn Fields
London WC2A 3PH
Tel: 020-7917 8888
Fax: 020-7955 0110
Website: www.landreg.gov.uk

LawNet
1st Floor
93-95 Bedford Street
Leamington Spa CV32 5BB
Tel: (01926) 886990
Fax: (01926) 886553
Website: www.lawnet.co.uk
Email: admin@lawnet.co.uk

Law Society of England and Wales
113 Chancery Lane
London WC2A 1PL
Tel: 020-7242 1222
Website: www.lawsociety.org.uk
*Provides names and addresses of solicitors.
Not an advisory service*

Law Society of Northern Ireland
Law Society House
98 Victoria Street
Belfast BT1 3JZ
Tel: 028-9023 1614
Fax: 028-9023 2606
Web: www.lawsoc-ni.org
Email: info@lawsoc-ni.org

Law Society of Scotland
26 Drumsheugh Gardens
Edinburgh EH3 7YR
Tel: 0131-226 7411
Fax: 0131-225 2934
Web: www.lawscot.org.uk
Email: lawscot@lawscot.org.uk

Legal Aid Department
Bedford House
16-22 Bedford Street
Belfast BT2 7FL
Tel: 028-9024 6441
Website: www.nilad.org

Legal Services Commission
85 Grays Inn Road
London WC1X 8TX
Tel: 020-7759 0000
Website: www.legalservices.gov.uk

Legal Services Ombudsman
3rd Floor
Sunlight House
Quay Street
Manchester M3 3JZ
Tel: (0845) 601 0794
Fax: 0161-832 5446
Website: www.olso.org
Email: lso@olso.gsi.gov.uk

London Lesbian and Gay Switchboard
Tel: 020-7837 7324 (24 hours)

London Women's Aid
PO Box 391
Bristol BS99 7WS
National helpline, tel: (0845) 702
3468 (24-hour helpline)
Website: www.womensaid.org.uk

Lord Chancellor's Department
54–60 Victoria Street
London SW1E 6QW
Tel: 020-7210 8500
Fax: 020-7210 0647
Email: enquiries@lcdhq.gsi.gov.uk
Website: www.open.gov.uk/lcd

Mediation Network for Northern Ireland
10 Upper Crescent
Belfast BT7 1NT
Tel: 028-9043 8614
Fax: 028-9031 4430
Email:
info@mediation-network.org.uk
Website:
www.mediation-network.org.uk

National Children's Bureau
8 Wakley Street
London EC1V 7QE
Tel: 020-7843 6000
Fax: 020-7278 9512
Email: library@ncb.org.uk
Website: www.ncb.org.uk

National Council for the Divorced and Separated
20 Newlands Avenue
Scunthorpe DN15 7HN
Tel: (07041) 478120
Email: info@ncds.org.uk
Website: www.ncds.org.uk
Has about 70 branches throughout the UK which provide a venue where people with similar experiences and problems can meet and develop new interests

National Council for One Parent Families
255 Kentish Town Road
London NW5 2LX
Tel: 020-7428 5400, (08000) 185026
Fax: 020-7482 4851
Email: info@oneparentfamilies.org.uk
Website: www.oneparentfamilies.org.uk

National Debtline
The Birmingham Settlement
318 Summer Lane
Birmingham B19 3RL
Tel: 0121-359 8501 (Mon, Thur 10-4; Tue, We 10-7; Fri 10-12)
Advice line, tel: (0645) 500511

National Family Mediation
9 Tavistock Place
London WC1H 9SN
Tel: 020-7383 5993
Fax: 020-7383 5994
Email: mediation@nfm.org.uk
Website: www.nfm.u-net.com

National Housing Federation
175 Grays Inn Road
London WC1X 8UP
Tel: 020-7278 6571
Fax: 020-7833 8323
Email: info@housing.org.uk
Website: www.housing.org.uk

Northern Ireland Housing Executive
Head Office
The Housing Centre
2 Adelaide Street
Belfast BT2 8PB
Tel: 028-9024 0588
Email: info@nihe.gov.uk
Website: www.nihe.gov.uk

Northern Ireland Women's Aid Federation
129 University Street
Belfast BT7 1HP
Tel: 028-9024 9358
Helpline, tel: 028-9033 1818 (24 hours)
Email: niwaf@dnet.co.uk
Website: www.niwaf.org

Office of Care and Protection
Royal Courts of Justice
PO Box 410, Chichester Street
Belfast BT1 3JF
Tel: 028-9072 4728
Fax: 028-9032 2782

Office of Fair Trading
PO Box 366
Hayes UB3 1XB
Tel: (0870) 606 0321
Fax: (0870) 607 0321
Email: enquiries@oft.gov.uk
Website: www.oft.gov.uk
Produces a number of free publications about personal finance, e.g. 'Debt – A Survival Guide' and 'No Credit'.

Office for National Statistics
General Register Office
Smedley Hydro
Trafalgar Road
Southport PR8 2HH
Certificate enquiries, tel: 0151-471 4800
Website: www.statistics.gov.uk

Office for the Supervision of Solicitors
Victoria Court
8 Dormer Place
Leamington Spa
Warwickshire CV32 5AE
Enquiry desk, tel: (01926) 820082
Helpline: (0845) 608 6565
Fax: (01926) 431435
Website: www.oss.lawsociety.org.uk

One Parent Families Scotland
13 Gayfield Square
Edinburgh EH1 3NX
Tel: 0131-556 3899/4563
Helpline: (08000) 185026
Fax: 0131-557 7899
Email: info@opfs.org.uk
Website: www.opfs.org.uk

Registers of Scotland Executive Agency
153 London Road
Edinburgh EH8 7AU
Tel: 0131-659 6111
Fax: 0131-479 3688
Email: keeper@ros.gov.uk
Website: www.ros.gov.uk

Relate National Marriage Guidance Council
Herbert Gray College
Little Church Street
Rugby
Warwickshire CV21 3AP
Tel: (01788) 573241
Fax: (01788) 535007
Email: enquiries@relate.org.uk
Website: www.relate.org.uk
Telephone numbers of local branches are listed in the telephone directory under 'Relate'

Relate Ireland
76 Dublin Road
Belfast BT2 7HP
Tel: 028-9032 3454
Fax: 028-9031 5298

Reunite (International Child Abduction Centre)
PO Box 24875
London E1 6FR
Tel: 020-7375 3440/3441
Fax: 020-7375 3442
Email: reunite@dircon.co.uk
Website: www.reunite.org

Scottish Legal Aid Board
44 Drumsheugh Gardens
Edinburgh EH3 7SW
Tel: 0131-226 7061
Fax: 0131-220 4878
Email: general@slab.org.uk
Website: www.slab.org.uk

Scottish Marriage Care
72 Waterloo Street
Glasgow G2 7DA
Tel: 0141-222 2166
Fax: 0141-222 2144
Email: info@scottishmarriagecare.co.uk
Website: www.scottishmarriagecare.co.uk

Scottish Women's Aid
Norton Park
57 Albion Road
Edinburgh EH7 5QY
Tel: 0131-475 2372
Fax: 0131-475 2384
Email: swa@swa-1.demon.co.uk
Website: www.scottishwomensaid.co.uk

Shelter National Campaign for the Homeless
88 Old Street
London EC1V 9HU
Helpline, tel: (0808) 800 4444 (24 hours)
Website: www.shelter.org.uk

Shelter Scotland
Ground Floor
Unit 2, Kittle Yards
Causewayside
Edinburgh EH9 1PJ
Tel: 0131-466 8031
Fax: 0131-466 8033
Website: www.shelterscotland.org.uk

Society of Pension Consultants
St Bartholomew House
92 Fleet Street
London EC4Y 1DG
Tel: 020-7353 1688
Fax: 020-7353 9296
Email: john.mortimer@spc.uk.com
Website: www.spc.uk.com

Solicitors Family Law Association
PO Box 302
Orpington
Kent BR6 8QX
Tel: (01689) 850227
Fax: (01689) 855833
Email: sfla@btinternet.com
Website: www.sfla.org.uk

Stonewall
46 Grosvenor Gardens
London SW1W 0EB
Tel: 020-7881 9440
Fax: 020-7881 9444
Email: info@stonewall.org.uk
Website: www.stonewall.org.uk
Organisation campaigning for gay and lesbian equality

UK College of Family Mediators
24–32 Stephenson Way
London NW1 2HX
Tel: 020-7391 9162
Fax: 020-7391 9165
Email: ukcfm@btclick.com
Website: www.ukcfm.co.uk

Women's Aid Federation for England
PO Box 391
Bristol BS99 7WS
Helpline: (0845) 702 3468
Email: web@womensaid.org.uk
Website: www.womensaid.org.uk

Useful websites
www.courtservice.gov.uk
www.divorce.co.uk
www.inlandrevenue.gov.uk
www.publictrust.gov.uk
www.nhsorgandonor.net

For insurance and pensions:
www.queercompany.com
www.thebignewcompany.com/
    massow
www.pinkfinance.com
www.bristol-west.co.uk

Index